TALKING T

CARIBBEAN ARCHAEOLOGY AND ETHNOHISTORY

L. Antonio Curet, Series Editor

TALKING TAÍNO

Essays on Caribbean Natural History from a Native Perspective

William F. Keegan
and
Lisabeth A. Carlson

THE UNIVERSITY OF ALABAMA PRESS
Tuscaloosa

Typeface: AGaramond

∞

The paper on which this book is printed meets the minimum requirements of
American National Standard for Information Sciences-Permanence of Paper for
Printed Library Materials, ANSI Z39.48-1984.

Library of Congress Cataloging-in-Publication Data

Keegan, William F.
Talking Taino : Caribbean natural history from a native perspective / William F.
Keegan and Lisabeth A. Carlson.
p.   cm. — (Caribbean archaeology and ethnohistory)
Includes bibliographical references and index.
ISBN 978-0-8173-1628-0 (cloth : alk. paper) — ISBN 978-0-8173-5508-1
(pbk. : alk. paper) — ISBN 978-0-8173-8076-2 (electronic : alk. paper)
1. Taino Indians—Antiquities. 2. Taino Indians—Social life and customs.
3. Taino Indians—First contact with Europeans. 4. West Indies—Antiquities.
I. Carlson, Lisabeth A. II. Title.
F1619.2.T3K45 2008
972.9004′97922—dc22
                                                                2008013999

Publication History
Most chapters were essays originally published in *Times of the Islands* (The International Magazine of the Turks & Caicos Islands) and were written by William
F. Keegan and/or Lisabeth A. Carlson, with the exception of "Birdland," which
was written by Carlson, Keegan, and David Steadman. "The Age of Reptiles" was
originally published as "Lizards and Snakes." "The First Documented Shark Attack in the Americas, circa AD 1000" was originally published on-line at http://
www.flmnh.ufl.edu/caribarch/sharks.htm. "Columbus, Hero or Heel?" and "One
Small Step for a Man" were originally published in the *VISTA* magazine's supplement to Sunday newspapers.

For Brian Riggs, friend, colleague, and inspiration

"If You Know Your History, Then You Will Know Where You're Coming From."
—Bob Marley

Contents

Illustrations

Plates

Preface

The gray beard (Bill, not Betsy) is telling. Combined, the two of us have spent forty-five years conducting archaeological research in the Caribbean. Bill started in 1978, and Betsy in 1992. Over the years we have directed research projects in Trinidad, Grenada, St. Lucia, Puerto Rico, the Dominican Republic, Haiti, Cuba, Jamaica, Grand Cayman, the Turks & Caicos Islands, and throughout the Bahamas. We have also had the good fortune to visit many of the other islands in the Caribbean.

Our experiences have been remarkable. We've walked hundreds of miles of Caribbean coastline, dodged drug smugglers, camped on beaches miles from humanity, seen the night sky in the total absence of other light, scuba dived in pristine waters, searched for glass fishing floats on beaches that no one ever visits, and enjoyed the wonders of nature that surrounded us. Most of all, wherever we went, we were welcomed by the friendly people who today live in these islands. It is an understatement to say that we were welcomed with open arms; it is more accurate to say that they adopted us!

The main reason we made these trips was to study the lifeways of the peoples who lived in the Caribbean before the arrival of Christopher Columbus. Sadly, harsh treatment and European diseases extinguished their culture, a culture we today call Taíno (also known as Arawak). In an effort to repay our debt to the past and the present we began writing a series of short essays called "Talking Taíno." The bottom line for each essay was showing the relationship between the Taínos of the past and the present natural history of the islands. Our goal has been to bring the past to life and to highlight commonalities between past and present. We did so by emphasizing Taíno words and beliefs about the natural world.

Most of the essays have a Taíno word list and English translation. The most comprehensive discussion of Caribbean languages was published by Julian Granberry and Gary Vescelius (2004). It should be noted that Taíno was not a written language, and thus there are a variety of spellings for the same word (e.g., zemí and cemí, Xaragua and Jaragua). The main issue is finding the letters that appropriately express particular pronunciations. In this regard, Granberry and Vescelius do an excellent job of capturing the proper pronunciation of Taíno words. Nevertheless, we have chosen some spellings included in Spanish publications that we feel better capture the Taíno language.

We encourage anyone who is interested in talking Taíno to consult the phonetic spellings provided in the book by Granberry and Vescelius, because the Spanish spellings for these words often yield pronunciations that would be spelled differently in English. For example, *gua* is pronounced wa; and the consonant *c* can have a hard or soft pronunciation (thus, *conuco* is pronounced konuko, while *cemí* is pronounced seme). Speaking the language requires specific knowledge of translation and pronunciation.

We initially wanted to call this collection "Buffalo Sojourn." The first meaning was a play on words that we hoped reggae fans would recognize immediately ("Buffalo Soldier"). A key line from Bob Marley's song is, "If you know your history, then you will know where you're coming from." Our intent in writing these essays was to provide a more detailed introduction to the natural history of the islands.

There was also a more personal connection. We began work on several archaeological research projects in the Turks & Caicos Islands in 1989, and were invited to Jamaica by Mr. Tony Clarke in 1998. One of our first (nonarchaeological) discoveries was that many of the feral donkeys that we had seen wandering the streets of Grand Turk had been airlifted to Jamaica, and were now thriving in the lush pastures of Tony's Paradise Park dairy farm. Tony was looking for an archaeologist to investigate the site on his property, and heard of us during the process of arranging the transfer of donkeys. We have worked for donkeys in the past, but this is the first time one got us a job! Several years later we encountered many new residents. Fidel Castro presented the prime minister of Jamaica with twelve water buffalos as a special gift in recognition of their many years of cooperation. This was a very practical gift, and it shows that heads of state are not always motivated by pomp and circumstance. But no water buffalo would want to live on the streets of Kingston, so they were distributed to several farms in the country, and four of them were sent to Paradise Park. The hope was that they would eat the water hyacinth that was clogging the Dean's Valley River, but they actually preferred pasture grass. We always thought that grass was grass, but these farms actually plant special pasture grasses for their dairy cows. The donkeys and water buffalos are thrilled! We spent five field seasons at Paradise Park working near our donkey friends from Grand Turk and the water buffalos from Cuba.

1. Feral donkeys on Grand Turk near North Wells. Photo by Lisabeth A. Carlson.

Very different worlds were thrust together into a common history five hundred years ago. We hope you will appreciate with us the wonders of the Caribbean world, the peoples who lived there in the past, and those who live there today. They are, whether you know it or not, an integral part of who you are.

Acknowledgments

There are far too many people to thank for their assistance on our various projects. First and foremost we met a strong and dedicated ally. Kathy Borsuk, managing editor of the International Magazine of the Turks & Caicos Islands, called *Times of the Islands,* embraced our concept. Most of the chapters in this book originally were published there. Kathy has created a phenomenal publication that reaches well beyond the Turks & Caicos Islands. We encourage everyone to subscribe, or at the very least, visit the magazine's web page: www.timespub.tc.

Most of these essays benefited greatly from discussions with our colleagues at the Florida Museum of Natural History. In particular, Dr. David Steadman (curator of Ornithology) coauthored one of the papers ("Birdland"). We appreciate his permission and willingness to include that essay in this collection and thank him for his permission to reproduce several of his photographs. We also appreciate the support of Dr. Douglas S. Jones, director of the Florida Museum of Natural History, for his support and permission to publish the shark attack essay that originally was published on the museum's web pages. Finally, *VISTA* magazine solicited articles on Columbus for their Sunday newspaper supplement. We appreciate their permission to include two of those here. We thank Dr. Peter Siegel for providing photos from the excavations at Maisabel, Puerto Rico, and we greatly appreciate the beautiful fish photographs provided by Barbara Shively and the artifact photographs provided by Corbett McP. Torrence.

We are especially fortunate that The University of Alabama Press found our work of sufficient interest to collect these writings in a book. It has been a pleasure to work with the staff at the press.

TALKING TAÍNO

Introduction

They are known today as Lucayan Taínos: an anglicized version of the Spanish "Lucayos," which derives from the Arawakan words *Lukkunu Kaíri* ("island men"). The Lucayans share a common ancestry with the Taíno societies of Puerto Rico, Haiti, the Dominican Republic, Cuba, and Jamaica (the Greater Antilles), who they separated from around AD 600 when they began to colonize the Turks & Caicos and The Bahamas (hereafter called the Lucayan Islands). By 1492, they had settled all of the larger Lucayan Islands. In addition, they continued to exchange goods with other Taínos living in the Greater Antilles.

To date, most of what has been written about the Taínos has drawn upon the written record left by the Spanish. However, because the chronicles were written to serve political objectives, be they for or against the native peoples, and because the chroniclers themselves were limited in their abilities to understand a nonwestern culture, these documents are rife with errors and misinformation. The uncritical use of the historical record has hampered efforts to understand native West Indian societies. For although we continue to speak of Taínos as a single unified group, there were regional differences in language and culture, if not also in race. One needs look only to the Soviet Union or the former Yugoslavia to be reminded of the fragility of national identities. This introduction draws on the last two decades of anthropological scholarship to present a brief chronicle of the development and extinction of Lucayan Taíno culture.

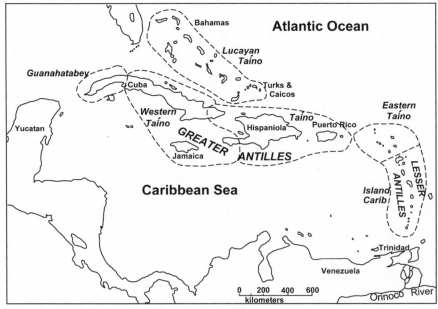

2. Map of the insular Caribbean showing culture areas.

Origins

The origins of the Lucayan Taínos are traced to the banks of the Orinoco River in Venezuela. As early as 2100 BC villages of horticulturalists who used pottery vessels to cook their food had been established along the Middle Orinoco. During the ensuing two millennia their population increased in numbers, and they expanded down river and outward along the Orinoco's tributaries to the coasts of Venezuela, the Guianas, and Trinidad. Their movements are easily traced because the pottery they manufactured is so distinctive. Called Saladoid after the archaeological site of Saladero, Venezuela, their vessels were decorated with white-on-red painted, modeled and incised, and crosshatched decorations (see plate 1).

Saladoid peoples expanded through the Antilles at a rapid pace. Because their earliest settlements, which date before 400 BC, are in the Leeward Islands, the Virgin Islands, and Puerto Rico, the inescapable conclusion is that most of the Lesser Antilles were leapfrogged in a direct jump from Venezuela/Trinidad to Puerto Rico and its neighbors. Moreover, the conditions, which stimulated the initial migration into the Antilles, continued to fuel dispersal from South America bringing a variety of related ethnic groups into the Antilles over the next millennium.

Saladoid peoples lived in small villages and practiced swidden agriculture in which a variety of different crops were cultivated in small gardens, a practice very similar to present-day "casual cultivation." Due to the limited fertility of the soil, gardens were cultivated for only a few years before new gardens had to be cleared. Frequent movement of village sites is evident from the absence of deeply stratified sites. A number of the early sites are located inland on watercourses adjacent to prime agricultural land, but most Saladoid sites are in coastal settings. In both settings, horticulture was the primary source of food. At the inland sites, land crab remains are the main component, while at coastal villages the shells of marine mollusks and bones of fishes were the most common food remains in the trash middens.

For some reason the Saladoid advance stalled after they had colonized eastern Hispaniola. Irving Rouse (1992) has suggested that a large and well-established population of hunter-gatherers barred their forward progress, and that the Saladoid population needed time to grow and refine their adaptation to island life before the frontier was breached. Some of the resident foragers may have been assimilated before further expansion took place.

The next phase of cultural development is announced by a marked change in material culture. Elaborate pottery decorations disappear, especially in frontier locations where most of the pottery was undecorated except for occasional red slip or simple modeling. These simplified designs have been classified as the Ostionoid series, named for the archaeological site of Punta Ostiones in western Puerto Rico. By AD 600 the "Ostionoid peoples" had resumed the advance of their Saladoid ancestors and had begun to expand along both coasts of Hispaniola. Expansion along the southern coast led to the colonization of Jamaica, while movement through the northern valleys led to the colonization of eastern Cuba, The Bahamas, and the Turks & Caicos.

Given the modern barren landscape of the Lucayan Islands it is often asked why anyone would leave the fertile valleys of the Greater Antilles to settle this island chain. The answer is that although the Lucayan Islands are today covered by low scrub vegetation and there is a noticeable lack of fresh water, these conditions did not prevail five hundred years ago. In fact, the Lucayan Islands would have been quite attractive to small groups of horticulturalists who farmed the loamy soils and relied on the sea for fish and transport.

Diet

Spanish records indicate that the Lucayan Taínos cultivated as many as fifty different plants, including varieties of sweet and bitter manioc, sweet potatoes, cocoyams, beans, gourds, chili peppers, corn, cotton, tobacco, bixa, genip, groundnuts, guava, and papaya. The carbonized remains of corn, chili peppers, palm fruits, unidentified tubers (probably manioc and sweet potato), and gourds are among the plant remains identified in West Indian sites. At least half of the Lucayan Taíno diet came from plant foods. Manioc (cassava) was the staple, followed by sweet potato. Corn was cultivated but apparently was of secondary importance.

Manioc tubers require special processing because they contain poisonous hydrocyanic acid. Sweet manioc has such small quantities of the poison it can be prepared like sweet potato—peeled and boiled. Bitter manioc, however, requires a more elaborate procedure which involves peeling, grinding or mashing, and squeezing the mash in a basket tube to remove the poisonous juices (see chapter 13). After the juice is removed the paste is dried and sieved for use as flour. Water is added to the flour to make the pancake-like cassava bread, which is cooked on a flat clay griddle. Fragments of these griddles and large ceramic bowls, both of which were made from red loam and crushed, burned conch shell, are common in Lucayan Island archaeological sites.

The poisonous manioc juice is not discarded. It is boiled to release the poison and then used as the liquid base for "pepper pot" stew. Adding chili peppers, other vegetables, meat, and fish to the simmering manioc juice makes pepper pot. This slow simmering stew allowed food that would otherwise spoil to be preserved and available for meals throughout the day. Today in South America, pepper pot is still eaten with cassava bread.

The other half of the diet came from creatures of the land and the sea. The few land animals that were available (iguana, crabs, and a cat-size rodent called hutia) were highly prized, but were only available in limited quantities. The major source of animal protein came from the coastal marine environment. Marine turtles and monk seals were available seasonally, but the main foods were the fishes and mollusks who feed in the grass flat/patch reef habitats between the barrier coral reef and the beach: parrotfish, grouper, snapper, bonefish, queen conch, urchins, nerites, chitons, and clams. Fish were captured with nets, basket traps, spears, bow and arrow, and weirs. The latter involved building check-dams across the mouths of tidal creeks, which allowed fishes to enter at high tide but prevented their escape when the tide changed. Meat and fish were grilled with leftovers added to the pepper pot.

When you consider the number of ways Lucayan Taínos could satisfy their hunger, the islands are noteworthy for the abundance of options. It is difficult to imagine that anyone ever went hungry, a conclusion confirmed by the preliminary examination of human skeletal remains, which indicate that the Lucayan Islanders enjoyed remarkably good health and nutrition. They certainly did not suffer from the nutritional and diet-related disorders that plagued other horticulturalists in the West Indies and elsewhere.

Society and Village Life

The Taínos lived in large multifamily houses. In Hispaniola there were two kinds of houses: the rectangular bohio and the round-to-oval caney, which had a high-pitched, conical thatched roof (see plate 2). Although a probable exaggeration, the early sixteenth-century Spanish chronicler Bartolomé de las Casas reported that some houses were occupied by 40 to 60 heads of household (roughly 250 men, women, and children). Households were formed around a group of related females. Grandmother, mother, sisters, and daughters lived together and cooperated in farming, childrearing, food preparation, and craft production. Men, by virtue of their absence from communities during periods of long-distance trade and/or warfare, were peripheral to the household. The importance of females as the foundation of society was expressed by tracing descent through the female line to a mythical female ancestress. This "matrilineal" social organization is common throughout the world.

The household's belongings were stored on the floors and in the rafters of the houses. Cotton hammocks for sleeping were strung between the central supports and eaves. Excavations of a house floor at a site in the Turks & Caicos Islands revealed ash deposits, which may have come from small, smoky fires used to control insect pests and to warm the house at night. Cooking was probably done in sheds outside the main house.

Most villages in the Lucayan Islands were composed of houses aligned atop a sand dune with the ocean in front and a marshy area behind. Quite likely, these marshy areas provided ready access to fresh water before the islands were deforested. In addition, many sites are located just offshore on small cays.

Lucayan Taíno sites often occur in pairs, which reflects either cooperation between socially allied communities or sequential settlements in the same location. The former possibility is more likely because it is the men who most often were the leaders, even in matrilineages, and especially with regard to external relations. In a matrilineal society, your mother's brother, and not your father, is the most important male in your life because he heads your family's lineage. However, if men are needed by their matrilineage, yet are expected to live in their wife's village, then social relations will be unstable. These competing demands can be balanced by establishing villages in close proximity, thus reducing the distances that men must travel to participate in their lineage affairs.

In the Greater Antilles a slightly different type of community plan predominates. Here the houses are arranged around central plazas. The plazas were used for public displays, ritual dances, recording astronomical events, and for the Taíno version of the ball game. The chief's house, typically located at one end of the plaza, stored the village idols and spirit representations called *cemís*.

Religion

The Taíno pantheon of *cemís* was divided by the dichotomies of gender and cultural/noncultural. There were principal male and female spirits of fruitfulness: *Yocahu*, the giver of manioc, and *Attabeira*, the mother goddess. They both were attended by twin spirits. *Maquetaurie Guayaba*, Lord of the Dead, and *Guabancex*, Mistress of the Hurricane, ruled the anti-cultural world. They too were attended by sets of twins. *Cemís* played an active role in the affairs of humans, and they served to distinguish between that which was human, cultural, and pleasing and that which was nonhuman, anti-cultural, and foul. But as exemplified by the twins, the Taínos recognized that the spirits of the world could simultaneously have positive and negative characteristics. For example, rains are good when they arrive at the right time and in the right quantity, but can also devastate agricultural lands when the timing is wrong or too much rain falls. The Taíno viewed their world in a delicate balance, and they attended to their spirits in order to maintain this balance.

Political Organization

By the time Europeans arrived, Taíno society had two main divisions. The rulers of the community were of a noble class (called *niTaínos*), which included chiefs, shamans, and other elites who held positions of authority. Chiefs (called *caciques*) ruled at several levels, from the paramount *caciques* that ruled large regions, to district leaders who were allied to a paramount, to headmen and clanlords who ruled at the village level. With noble birth being the main prerequisite of this rank, it should be noted that women could also be chiefs. Between *caciques* of all levels, alliances were formed through marriages.

Supporting the rulers were large numbers of commoners. Blood and marriage (kinship) were the threads that bound commoners to caciques. There was also a level below the commoner class, which the Spanish described as a class of servants called *naborias*. *Naborias* were once thought to be slaves, but a careful reading of the early Spanish chronicles indicates that they served through a sense of obligation and were not chattel.

Caciques organized villages into regional polities who competed with one another for a variety of resources. There is increasing evidence that, contrary to the "peaceful Arawak" stereotype, the Taíno chiefdoms made war on one another prior to the arrival of the Spanish.

Caciques also organized long-distance trade. Travel between islands was accomplished in canoes dug out of a single log, the largest of which could carry approximately ninety passengers. Traders sought both domestic trade items (salt, dried fish, and conch) and exotic materials from other chiefdoms and from neighboring islands. The red jewel box shell (*Chama sarda*) disk beads that were manufactured throughout the Lucayan Islands are an example of an exotic good. These beads were woven into belts that served to record alliances between chiefdoms. These and other exotic materials served to reinforce the authority of the *caciques* to whom access to these goods was restricted. By one account, Taíno *caciques* held authority of life or death over their subjects.

Warfare

When Columbus set foot on the island he called San Salvador, young men carrying spears who were there to defend their village met him. Other encounters between the Spanish and the Taínos also point to the importance of warfare in Taíno society. For instance, when Columbus embarked on the conquest of central Hispaniola in 1494 he was challenged by an army of up to fifteen thousand warriors (although this may have been an exaggeration). Moreover, shortly after the Spanish arrested Caonabo, the *cacique* of the central Hispaniola region of Maguana, Bartholomew Columbus was passing along the Neiba River, which formed the boundary between the regions of Xaragua and Maguana. Here he encountered an army from Xaragua that was probably in the area to co-opt villages that had previously been allied with the deposed Chief Caonabó. Taíno social organization also points to the presence of an organized and well-armed militia.

Genocide

Within a generation of the arrival of the Spanish, the native peoples of the Lucayan Islands were extinct. In 1513, Juan Ponce de Leon sailed through the Lucayan Islands on his way to Florida. He reported that he encountered only one inhabitant, an old native man still living in the Turks & Caicos Islands. Other expeditions followed, including two in 1520, which failed to encounter any native peoples in these islands.

The fate of the Lucayan Taínos can be traced to the mines on Hispaniola and to the pearl beds of Cubagua Island off the coast of Venezuela. By 1509, the Spanish governor of Santo Domingo had convinced King Ferdinand that there was a critical shortage of labor on Hispaniola. In response the king ordered that all peoples from the neighboring islands be relocated to Hispaniola. A slaving consortium was soon formed in Concepcion de la Vega, although documents in the archives in Seville suggest that the practice of enslaving Lucayans had begun much earlier. The contact period Spanish chronicler Peter Martyr D'Anghera reported that forty thousand Lucayans were brought to Hispaniola. The total population of the islands was probably twice that number when children, old people, and others who died are included. A total population of forty to eighty thousand Lucayans is consistent with archaeological deposits in these islands.

When Columbus landed at Guanahaní in 1492 he was met by people whose simple dress and material technology belied their social and political complexity. Theirs was a vibrant culture in the process of filling up the northern and western Lucayan Islands at the same time they were competing among themselves for political and economic control of the central islands. Moreover, had the Spanish never arrived, the Lucayan Taínos might soon have been subject to demands from the Classic Taínos on Hispaniola who were already establishing bases or outposts in the Turks & Caicos and Great Inagua by the middle of the thirteenth century. Instead, the Lucayan Taínos are remembered as the first native peoples to challenge Columbus and the first to be extinguished.

I
The Spanish Translation

The real voyage of discovery consists not in finding new lands but in seeing with new eyes.

—Marcel Proust

Christopher Columbus is a provocative character. His is not the biography of an ordinary man; his is the story of a symbol whose fortunes have crested and fallen over the past five centuries. He went from the first successful transatlantic voyage, to a penniless death in 1506, to heroic status as a symbol for the United States as it emerged on the world stage with the Columbian Exposition in Chicago (1893), to the murderer of all native peoples during the Columbus Quincentenary. Who says history is dead?

Columbus achieved legendary status thanks to a largely fictional biography published by Washington Irving in 1892. Washington Irving is best known for his stories of Rip Van Winkle and the headless horseman ("The Legend of Sleepy Hollow"). Contrary to Irving's assertions, Queen Isabel didn't hock her jewels, there were not two logs of the voyage, the crew did not threaten mutiny, and "landfall" was not made on October 12 (it was made on the eleventh). Just about everything else Irving wrote about the first voyage are half-truths and postures. When you're creating a hero, you can't let the truth get in your way.

Another aspect of this story that is equally inaccurate is the portrayal of the native people who met Columbus. Much of the history of these peoples is based on what Columbus wrote about them. Imagine if someone who didn't understand your language or culture (and who never met "you," but knew his ways were far superior to yours) wrote about you—and five hundred years later everyone still believed him! Remember also that in describing this New World, Columbus was try-

TAÍNO WORD	TRANSLATION
Taíno	Noble or good person
Ni Taíno	Elites or noble class
Lucairi	Island people
Cayo	Cay (or small island)
Caico	Outer or faraway island
Ciboney	Peoples of central Cuba
Ciba	Stone or stony
Guanahatabey	Peoples of western Cuba
Guanahacabibe	Small land of caves
Cacicazgo	Chiefdom
Cacique	Chief
Caribe	Strong or brave person
Canoa	Canoe
Huracan	Hurricane
Hamaca	Hammock
Cemí	Deity
Barbacoa	Barbecue

ing to convince his king and queen that these lands were of such abundance that the sovereigns should underwrite the cost of their exploitation and colonization.

Columbus gave new names to many of the places he landed. For example, the Lucayan Islanders called the island where Columbus first landed *Guanahaní,* but Columbus called it San Salvador (which translates as "Holy Savior"). To make matters worse, Columbus asserted that the native peoples owed allegiance to the Spanish monarchs. Imagine how we would react today if a foreign power from across the ocean landed on our shores, gave our country a new name, and demanded that we change our system of government!

All forms of communication must be interpreted in context. How do people who do not understand one another's language communicate? How much credibility should be given to the written language in which such encounters were recorded? Can we recognize the biases of the people who wrote the story and juxtapose these to the biases of the people they encountered? Can we read between the lines?

So, what do we know about the native peoples of the West Indies that we learned from the early Spanish explorers? We do know that in some places they used the

3. Columbus claiming possession of his first landfall in the Bahamas (*Guanahaní*).

word *Taíno* when greeting the Spanish. The word is translated as "noble" or "good," and is the root of the word *niTaíno,* which was used in reference to the noble or elite class of Taíno society. Taíno has replaced the earlier term "Arawak" as the most commonly used name to identify the pre-Columbian inhabitants of the central Caribbean islands just before and at the time of European contact.

In 1871, the American ethnologist Daniel Brinton suggested that we call these people "Island Arawaks." After researching native West Indian words recorded by the Spanish, Brinton recognized that the Taíno spoke a language that belonged to the Arawakan family of languages common in South America. Because he understood that these people were different from the mainland Arawaks, Brinton included the prefix "Island" in his designation. Yet, over the years the prefix was dropped for simplicity. By the mid-1980s, archaeologists had realized that using the name Arawak (without the Island) had blurred distinctions between South American and West Indian natives, so they adopted the term *Taíno.*

Of course, the West Indian natives had many regional names for themselves and the Spanish recorded some of these. The Spanish called the islands to the north of Hispaniola "Las Islas de Los Lucayos," and so we call the native peoples of the Bahama archipelago the "Lucayans" (or more accurately "Lucayan Taínos"). "Lucayo" ultimately came from the Taíno words *lu,* which means tribe or people, and *cairi,* which translates as island. So the Lucayan Taínos are "good island people." Our word cay (or key) comes from another Taíno word for a small island, *cayo,* and the word *caico* means outer island or faraway island.

The Dominican friar Bartolomé de las Casas described a number of culturally distinct groups in the Greater Antilles in the early sixteenth century. Among these were the *Ciboney* (also spelled Siboneyes) of central Cuba, who Las Casas indicated were being enslaved by Hispaniolan Taínos who had settled on the island. The Taíno word *ciba* translates as stony or rocky in this context and likely refers to the topography of central Cuba. In the past, archaeologists have mistakenly used Ciboney to refer to the pre-Taíno (Archaic Age) peoples of Cuba. The Archaic Age (circa 5000 BC to AD 500) peoples supposedly did not make pottery or practice agriculture, yet Las Casas was clear in stating that the Ciboney were culturally very similar to the Lucayans who were ceramic-producing farmers.

There does exist the possibility that Archaic Age peoples were still living in far-western Cuba when the Spanish arrived. However, these people are more accurately called *Guanahatabey* or *Guanahacabibe,* names given to them by the Taínos. Although there were no firsthand accounts of the Guanahatabey, Las Casas described them as cave dwellers who came out only to hunt and fish. To add to the confusion, the mythological ancestors of the Taíno were described in much the same way. *Cabibe* is the Taíno word for cave and the term *Guanahacabibe* roughly translates as "small land of caves." Guanahacabibe was also the name of the westernmost Cuban chiefdom (*cacicazgo*), which is a political region ruled by a single powerful *cacique.* This chiefdom type of government is now recognized as having occurred worldwide, and its development is one of the main subjects of archaeological inquiry. For now, we currently lack reliable information on when people were living in western Cuba, their cultural affiliation, and, ultimately, even whether the Guanahatabey were real or mythical beings.

The last major group of native West Indians is the Caribs. These are the people Columbus described as cannibals, keeping in mind that "cannibals" were allowed by Queen Isabel to be taken as slaves. Practically, this designation was used as a justification for the mistreatment of the native populations. The Taíno had cannibals (*caribe*) in their mythology, as well, but they had not ever encountered any in person (see chapter 19). In the Taíno language *Caribe* translates as any strong or brave person. As far as archaeologists are concerned, the Island Caribs were Arawakan-speaking peoples who came from South America, occupied the Windward Islands of the Lesser Antilles late in the pre-Columbian period, and survived well into historic times. They did not practice cannibalism.

Columbus recorded some aspects of the everyday lives of the people he first encountered in these islands, and some Taíno words have survived and are part of our modern English vocabulary. The following introduces the most commonly used Taíno words in the English language. Being a sailor, Columbus was greatly impressed by the local boats. Taínos called their dugout boats *canoa* (canoe). They could hold up to ninety men and could be paddled almost as fast as a Spanish caravel could sail (about six knots)! A *canoa* was hewn from a single log using fire to char the wood and stone or shell tools to hollow out the log. Columbus observed very large canoes with brightly painted bow and sternposts housed in special sheds on the beach in south Cuba. Surprisingly the Taínos apparently never used sails on their dugouts.

A major threat to seafaring in the West Indies is hurricanes. The name is derived from the Taíno word *huracan*. In Taíno imagery, a common depiction is a bodiless circular head with two hands spiraling off it in opposite directions. This is possibly an image of the *cemí* who controls hurricanes, exhibiting a simple expression of the counterclockwise action at the center of a hurricane.

Another everyday Taíno item is the *hamaca*. Hammocks were woven from native cotton, century plant, and sisal fibers—three Taíno plants that were first observed and described by the Spanish. These net beds were strung between the center and wall posts of the houses and are essential tropical climate gear. They transformed European sea travel by providing a comfortable accommodation for sleeping aboard ship.

Because meats spoil quickly in tropical climates, the Taíno practiced two basic techniques for storing meats: "corning" (salting) and drying/smoking. The Taíno placed fish and meat on a wooden lattice and roasted or smoked them over an open fire. The Spanish called this grill a *barbacoa,* from which we get our word barbecue.

An interesting aside is that this name was given to European peoples who roamed the Caribbean in the seventeenth century and were called "buccaneers." They have come to be identified as pirates, yet the buccaneers were not pirates. As the historian Richard Pares (1963) noted in his history of war and trade in the West Indies, "In its origin a buccaneer was a landsman who hunted cattle and not a seaman who hunted Spaniards." These "cow-killers" preyed on wild cattle and pigs that flourished on depopulated lands. The name derived from their practice of roasting or drying meat on a grill over an open fire. They were "a voluntary community of stateless persons" that attracted all kinds of uprooted individuals from all nations. Buccaneers lived in out-of-the-way places where they cut mahogany trees; fished for sea turtle to acquire hawksbill shell; procured dyewoods; gathered sarsaparilla, vanilla, silk grass, and annatto; and engaged in contraband trade with the Spanish.

Their heyday lasted less than a century. They were the original mobile labor force in the islands; they went wherever they could make an honest living. Such mobility is still observed today throughout the islands (just ask Western Union).

It is surprising how much we do know about the Taíno considering that by 1524 they no longer existed as a separate population group. They left a legacy of food crops and cultural items that are enjoyed today. Even through the eyes of the Spanish, part of the inner life of this lost culture was captured and can be imagined these five hundred years later.

2
Starry, Starry Night

Jacques Derrida is dead. He died on October 9, 2004, at the age of seventy-four. Derrida was a French philosopher who recognized the importance of language in shaping our perception of the world around us. He pioneered a field of critical theory called deconstructionism. The approach argues that all writing has multiple layers of meaning, which even the author might not understand. Written language is thus open to an endless process of reinterpretation. It can be compared to peeling back the layers of an onion.

This collection of essays is all about Taíno language. For the most part we will deal with words that name particular plants, animals, and activities; but we will try to show the ways in which Taíno beliefs, myths if you will, structured the meanings of particular species and behaviors. We are constrained by the fact that the Taínos did not have a written language, which means we must rely on the Spanish chroniclers for the Taíno words that had importance and meaning. They are translations that cannot possibly capture the meanings that were understood by native speakers.

Vincent van Gogh is also dead. He died a long time ago (1890), but he left a lasting mark on the world. His schizophrenia shaped an artistic palette that distorted the colors and hues that the "normal" brain perceives. One of the most acclaimed paintings of this postimpressionist artist is titled "The Starry Night." In it, and in his other works, he depicts things that the rest of us do not see.

Derrida and van Gogh remind us that we live in a world of language and impressions, and that these may not fit our own modern beliefs or interpretations of

TAÍNO WORD	TRANSLATION
Jejen (Maye)	Mosquito
Turey	Sky, gold, heavenly
Mani (Cacahuete)	Peanut
Opía	Spirit of the dead
Cobo	Conch shell
Cuyo	Light
Karaya	Moon

the natural world. We tend to look at the world according to what we read and see; yet looking beyond what we usually see to that which we don't see can enrich our lives. One of the most impressive things that we no longer see is the starry night.

Sitting on the beach at Jacksonville Harbour on the uninhabited island of East Caicos in the Turks & Caicos Islands, we were finishing our one-pot meal of Thai chicken in peanut sauce that had been cooked on a small gas stove when we began to detect a humming in the bush behind us. As the sound grew in intensity we dove for our tents as swarms of mosquitoes (the Taíno called them *jejen* or *maye*) descended upon us. Trapped in our nylon cocoons we waited impatiently. Two hours later we emerged to a new world. Most of the mosquitoes had gone to bed, and we were immersed in the glow of starlight. Our surroundings were dominated by the brilliance of the heavens. The Taíno word for sky was *turey*. This also was the Taíno word for the brass objects brought by the Europeans, which were so shiny and brilliant that they must have come from the heavens.

It is likely that similar scenes were played out every day for hundreds of years by the Taíno peoples who inhabited these islands (although they didn't have Thai chicken for dinner, they did grow peanuts, which they called *mani* or *cacahuete*). The darkness of the surrounding forest was a dangerous place at night where *opía* (spirits of the dead) wandered, eating guavas and sweet fruits while searching for the living. But the village was far from dark. The night only seems dark to those who find incandescent lights a necessity. As John Denver wrote in his song "Rocky Mountain High," "the shadows from the starlight were softer than a lullaby." You have to experience it to believe him.

Although the nighttime held particular dangers, it also provided opportunities. Taínos paddling a canoe from the Turks & Caicos Islands to Hispaniola during the day would run out of visual landmarks soon after passing Bush Cay. Bush Cay is five miles south of Big Ambergris Cay on the Turks Bank, within the Seal Cays

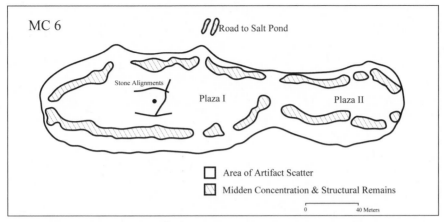

4. MC-6 site map showing plazas surrounded by midden concentrations and structural remains. Stone alignments shown in center of Plaza I. Redrawn after Sullivan (1981).

Wildlife Sanctuary. However, the night sky offered thousands of points of reference. It has long been the ideal map for sailors.

The night sky also offers a more encompassing display by which the passing of the seasons can be observed. It is true that the sun provided some hint of the passing of time, but the night sky is superior in this regard.

Dr. Shaun Sullivan pioneered the study of Lucayan Taíno astronomy in the late 1970s during his research at the archaeological site of MC-6 on the south coast of Middle Caicos. At the middle of the site he found a stone-lined courtyard (see plate 3). This court is a remarkable piece of engineering. It is virtually flat, exhibiting only ten centimeters (four inches) of grade despite five hundred years of weathering. It was constructed with soil carried from the salina along the south side of the site. The northern and southern margins of the court are flanked by double rows of undressed limestone that are incorporated into earthen ridges. Sullivan's topographic map showed that the double rows of stones were not parallel but instead bowed proportionately along their course. The court is about thirteen meters (forty-two feet) wide at either end, and at the middle it is about nineteen meters (sixty-two feet) wide. In addition, there is a large stone, with a depression at its center, which had been set in the center of the court.

The rest of the settlement is organized around the court. There are eight structures with stone foundations surrounding the court. Sullivan found that when a transit was positioned over the central stone and then pointed at a structure mound on the periphery of the plaza, turning the transit 180 degrees intersected a com-

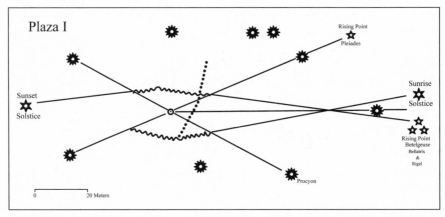

5. Alignments at MC-6 between the east-west stone alignments, the central stone, and the structural foundations surrounding the plaza as they relate to the rising and setting of the summer solstice sun and various stars. A third stone alignment is shown crossing the plaza south to north. Redrawn after Sullivan (1981).

plementary structure mound on the other side of the plaza. In addition, two other stone foundations were precisely reciprocal in that both had prominent high points on the side toward the plaza. When the transit was set over the central stone and the crosshairs centered on the midpoint of one of the structural prominences and then flipped, the prominence of the reciprocal structure was bisected precisely. The prominences were not functionally integral to the structures to which they were attached. They seem to have been used for some manner of sight alignment.

The main alignment through the center of the court conforms to the rising and setting sun on the summer solstice, an event that Sullivan observed firsthand in 1981. Sullivan also identified a number of other alignments with the rising and setting of stars that are significant in Native American astronomy, the most significant of which are alignments with the rising and setting positions of Betelgeuse, one of the principal stars in the constellation Orion. This court served as a link to the heavens as an observatory that could mark important cosmological events.

Orion is located on the celestial equator and has three of the twenty-five brightest stars in the night sky (Betelgeuse, Bellatrix, and Rigel). The stars of Orion are brilliant even in a night sky diminished by modern light pollution. Because the belt of Orion is aligned with the celestial equator and sits at the center of the tropical sky, it has served as an important constellation in native South American cosmologies. For many South American cultures, Orion was not a hunter but rather the "one-legged man."

Orion follows a cycle that provides an obvious means for telling time and mark-

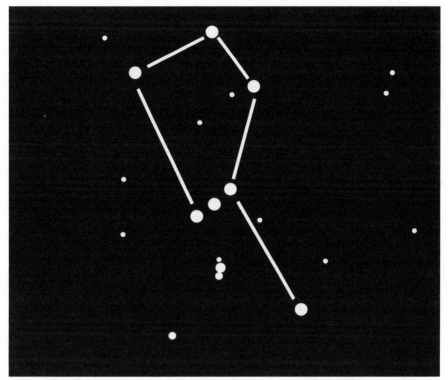

6. Drawing of constellation Orion with lines added to depict the "one-legged man," its representation in many native South American cosmologies.

ing the seasons. It makes its first appearance low on the horizon at dawn in early July and appears higher and higher each morning until mid-September when it is at the center of the sky at dawn. By mid-December, Orion sits at the center of the midnight sky. By mid-March, it is at the center of the sky at sunset, after which it appears lower and lower on the horizon each sunset until disappearing in late May. In this way, Orion can act as a marker for the summer and winter solstices and the vernal equinox. One reason for using Orion is that its circuit through the sky marks the beginning and end of the wet and dry seasons so important for tropical farmers. Orion's position can also indicate periods of good and bad fishing.

For the Taíno, Orion had a mythical identity in the guise of *Anacacuya*. According to the Taíno myth recorded by Ramón Pané in 1496 in northwest Hispaniola, Anacacuya was a prominent *cacique* who was drowned by his brother-in-law *Guayahona,* because Guayahona wanted to take all the women of the village for himself. While on a canoe trip, Guayahona told Anacacuya to look closely at a beautiful *cobo* or seashell in the water (likely a large conch), and then toppled him into the sea where he drowned. Each night, stars set into the sea and are born from the sea. Through the water, Anacacuya was able to enter the supernatural world of the sky and become Orion. *Cuyo* means "light" and Anacacuya literally translates as "light at the center."

Just like Anacacuya, the night sky rises at dusk from the sea and sets back into the ocean at dawn. The Taíno word for moon was *karaya*. The best time to watch the full moon rise over the ocean is not actually on the night of the full moon, since the full moon rises at sunset when the sky is not fully dark. The night following the full moon rise, you will see the still full moon rise from a dark ocean one hour after sunset. On many of the small Caribbean islands it is possible with a little effort to watch both the rise and fall of the moon and stars directly into the sea.

Here, it is possible to get a sense of the experience of the premodern world by observing the night sky. In most places this has become impossible due to light pollution. We no longer live in places where the horizon is completely dark at night. Yet, on many Caribbean islands one can still find places to observe the stars in complete darkness. Experiencing this gives a truer appreciation of the role that the night sky played in the lives of the people who first lived in the islands and a clearer vision of the starry, starry night.

3
Sharks and Rays

When the Spanish invaded the Americas, they quite literally landed in a New World. Like Dorothy in Oz, exotic and unknown peoples, plants, and animals surrounded them, and they struggled to find the words to describe them. One can imagine the Spanish pointing at various things and asking, "¿Como se dice? (What is it called?)." As with all languages, when an object or idea is new, the native term is frequently adopted. Granberry and Vescelius's studies have shown that the people in the Lucayan Islands spoke the Taíno language.

As the Lucayan Taínos were related to the Taínos of the Greater Antilles, Taíno outposts or colonies occurred in the southernmost Lucayan Islands. Outposts have been identified in the Turks & Caicos Islands on Grand Turk (occupied from the eighth through the thirteenth centuries) and on Middle Caicos (occupied during the fifteenth century).

Luis Hernández Aquino scoured more than 150 sources dealing with the initial contact period in the West Indies to compile a dictionary of Taíno words. The second edition of his dictionary of indigenous, mostly Taíno, words was published in 1977. The book is a fascinating portal to the world of the Taínos. As might be expected, most of the words are names for people and places or for plants and animals. Clearly, the dictionary is biased toward people and things the Spanish deemed worthy of mention, and although the dictionary focuses on Puerto Rico, many of the words can be applied to plants and animals across the Caribbean.

Each of these essays discusses a different aspect of the Taíno's natural world. We

TAÍNO WORD	TRANSLATION
Libuza	Southern stingray
Chucho	Spotted eagle ray
Hagueta	Small shark
Carite	Tiger shark
Cajaya	Bull shark
Caconeta	Shark
Cacona	Reward

incorporate as much of the Taíno language as possible in describing these land-scapes. Along the way, you might also learn to speak a little Taíno.

The Taínos, and especially the Lucayan Taínos, were maritime peoples. Not only were their villages located on the coast, they also consumed large quantities of fish and shellfish. In fact, one way to read the Taíno origin myth is: "In the beginning, God created fish" (see chapter 9). With all of the time they spent in and on the water, it is not surprising that the most dangerous and most exotic animals attracted their attention. The Taínos had at least four words for sharks, and they recognized both the bottom-dwelling southern stingray (*libuza*) and the elegant spotted eagle ray (*chucho*). The remains of sharks and rays are found in virtually every archaeological site in the region. Many of the bones of sharks and rays are made of cartilage, which do not preserve in archaeological sites. However, the vertebrae and teeth of sharks are commonly preserved, as are the vertebrae and barbed spine located at the base of a stingray's tail and the grinding plates in the mouth of a spotted eagle ray (see plate 4).

Southern stingrays played an important role in the Taíno economy by providing the source material for speartips used both in hunting and fishing and in warfare. Columbus reported that the Taíno tipped their spears with "the tooth of a fish." It is likely that what Columbus was describing was the spine that tips the stingray's tail. These barbed spines have been recovered in archaeological deposits and some show evidence for use, including shaped bases for hafting and dulled ends of the points. Stingray-spine tipped spears and arrows also were used as weapons. At the Maisabel site on the north coast of Puerto Rico, Dr. Peter Siegel (1992) excavated a human burial in which the individual had a stingray spine lodged in his rib cage, a wound that apparently caused his death.

A final, and quite remarkable, use of the southern stingray involved its skin. The Spanish reported "a large saltwater fish whose dark skin used to be used by the Indians over a rock, due to its roughness, in order to scratch cassava and to produce a very fine farina with which they used to make the best round cakes of cassava"(Oviedo 1526). Some stingray species have a row of placoid scales running along the midline of the back, which could be used to "scratch" the manioc to a fine pulp.

Sharks were another significant economic resource for the Taínos, providing meat and raw materials for tools and decorative items. The Taínos had numerous words to describe sharks. *Hagueta* refers to small sharks of various species. Small sharks were commonly harvested from inshore, shallow waters and, where available, were a staple of the Taíno subsistence. *Hagueta* probably simply refers to shark as an ordinary food item. The other names for sharks are *caconeta, cajaya,* and *carite.* These words are similar and all refer to large, dangerous sharks.

Carite is a tiger shark, the fiercest predator in the ocean that the Taíno were likely to encounter. These solitary predators cruise all areas of deep water and in-shore environments and can be quite aggressive to humans. The word *carite* is similar to the Taíno word for their enemies from the Lesser Antilles, the *Caribe.* As previously mentioned, *Caribe* describes a "strong or brave person." Both *carite* and the *Caribe* were elements of the Taíno world that they preferred not to encounter. The archaeological site of Maisabel again provides an interesting case. Dr. Siegel found another skeleton that was virtually complete; all that was missing was the lower right arm. On the upper arm bone there were unusually sharp cut marks. At first it was thought that this person had been injured in a battle. On close exami-nation, experts concluded that the cut marks had been made by a tiger shark (see chapter 4).

Cajaya is the Taíno name for bull sharks. Bull sharks inhabit the inshore waters and coral reefs surrounding these islands, hunting in the same fishing grounds used by the Taíno. They also commonly enter freshwater environments. Encountering a bull shark, or *cajaya,* would have been a common occurrence. According to George Burgess, director of the International Shark Attack File kept at the Florida Museum of Natural History, bull sharks are responsible for the largest number of recorded shark attacks across the globe.

The final term for shark is *caconeta.* The root word *cacona* means "reward"; therefore, a *caconeta* may refer to a captured adult shark. A harvested shark would have brought many rewards to its captor. In addition to the immense amount of meat, the shark's teeth, skin, and vertebrae were used as tools, weapons, and deco-ration.

Some shark teeth found in archaeological sites appear to have been used as drills; some have been modified to fit in handles; and others have holes drilled in the tooth root (see plate 5). People often jump to the conclusion that a drilled hole must mean that the teeth were jewelry. It is possible some Taínos wore these items to show their might or to protect them from death. But in other cases, modification allowed the tooth to be attached to a handle. Prior to the introduction of metal tools by the Spanish there were very few sources of sharp tools. Shark teeth would have made excellent cutting tools; they might even have been used as spear or arrow points. Sharkskin, like the stingray skin, is rough like sandpaper and was used to work and polish wood, shell, and bone.

It is clear that many names were necessary to distinguish the different roles sharks and rays played in the lives of the Taíno. The subtleties of the names provide a window to their lives and their natural landscapes.

4
First Documented Shark Attack in the Americas, Circa AD 1000

There are no eyewitness accounts, only the testimony of the bones. Yet our knowledge of prehistoric lifeways and forensic anthropology allow us to reconstruct what probably happened. The incident went something like this:

Their village was on the north coast of Puerto Rico near the modern town of Vega Baja. The two fishermen left the village as the sun was rising in the east. They pushed their small dugout canoe into the gentle surf and began paddling toward the azure reef line about five hundred meters from shore. Small whitecaps broke on the reef marking their destination. They were probably using hook and line, spears, or a net, or possibly all three, depending on the conditions that day and the fish they were encountering. Their prey were the groupers, snappers, parrotfishes, and grunts that live in close association with the reef. Then suddenly, their world was turned upside down.

There was no soundtrack music to raise the alarm, just the gentle lapping of waves on the side of the canoe as it bobbed gently in the light chop generated by the shallow reef. It was likely a beautiful morning, with high cumulous clouds in a robin's egg blue sky and golden rays of sunlight projected by the dawn, a morning of peace and beauty and perhaps a bountiful catch.

They had hooked and likely speared several fish, which they discussed in animated voices. The thrill of the hunt and the joy of success were celebrated. There were sharp pulls on the cotton handline. The fisherman reached with his right arm over the side of the dugout. But before he could free his catch, a monster rose out of the depths. The tiger shark, attracted by blood from the bleeding fish, bit sharply into the fisherman's upper arm and began its death roll. Failing to sever the upper arm at midshaft, it tore the flesh from his arm as its razor-sharp teeth descended toward the elbow. At the elbow the strength of its bite and the violent twisting of its body ripped the lower arm cleanly away. Blood gushed from the amputated extremity.

The canoe may have capsized, or the fisherman may have simply collapsed on its floor, his blood mixing with that of their catch. Without modern medical assistance, his life drained away. His partner succeeded in righting and guiding the canoe back to shore. With the assistance of other men who came racing from the village to see what had happened, they carried him home. His body was buried in the middle of the village, under the plaza. The cleared space at the center of the community where people gathered in communal events. There was great sadness at the loss of this adult man, the head of a family and able provider of fish for his village. His burial placed him among the ancestors. Although he was gone from this world, he lived on in the world of the dead where he could forever be called upon to help when assistance from the otherworld was needed.

Although this re-creation of an event that took place more than one thousand years ago is somewhat fanciful and perhaps even melodramatic, it fits what we know of life in pre-Columbian Puerto Rico.

In the late 1980s, Peter Siegel, with support from the Centro de Investigaciones Indigenas de Puerto Rico, directed archaeological excavations at the pre-Columbian site known as Maisabel on the north coast of Puerto Rico near the modern town of Vega Baja. The research was the basis for his Ph.D. dissertation (Siegel 1992). Dr. Siegel found that the site had been occupied from around 120 BC until AD 1000, making it one of the earliest and longest-lived villages in the West Indies. The site is composed of six middens (deposits of pottery, food remains, and other artifacts) arranged in a roughly circular shape. The middens surround a plaza in which very few artifacts were found. However, during the excavations Siegel discovered that the plaza was a large cemetery. He describes this central plaza as the *axis mundi,* the central axis of the world, in the eyes of the people who created it. This *axis mundi* served to connect the various layers of the cosmos (sky, land, and subterranean waters). At the most basic level the cemetery held the bones of the ancestors, who were venerated by their living descendants.

Dr. Siegel enlisted the assistance of Linda Budinoff, a graduate student studying human remains, for the analysis of the skeletons that he excavated. Her conclusions were presented at the Twelfth International Congress of the International Association for Caribbean Archaeology in Cayenne, French Guiana, and were published in the Proceedings of the Congress (1991). Burial number 17 turned out to

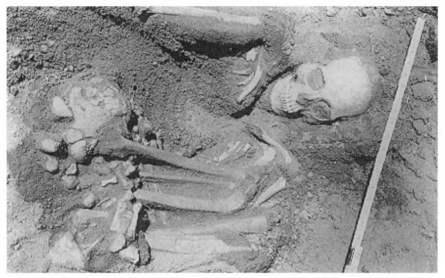

7. Burial number 17, a twenty-nine-year-old male who was fatally attacked by a tiger shark more than one thousand years ago. Photo by Peter E. Siegel (used by permission).

be of special interest. According to her analysis, burial 17 was a twenty-nine-year-old male. He was buried in a flexed (fetal) position, with prehistoric pottery, chert flakes, unmodified raw local stone, shell, chert hammerstone, calcite, ochre, and a coral abrader. The skeleton is complete with the exception of the lower right arm and hand. There are a series of cut marks on the upper right arm (humerus), which Budinoff says could indicate he "may have been tortured and executed" (118). One radiocarbon date places the time of death sometime between cal AD 789 and 1033. This skeleton, along with another that had a stingray spine lodged between its ribs, were used as evidence for armed conflict at the time.

The characteristics of the multiple cut marks led Keegan to question whether they were actually caused by a weapon. For instance, the marks occur on opposite sides of the bone with all of the cuts in a downward (distal) direction. One can easily envision someone being struck in such a way on the outer part of his arm, but it is difficult to imagine how similar cuts were made on the inner arm near the body. If the arm was raised when the blows were struck, then the cuts would occur in an upward direction toward the proximal end of the humerus. In other words, the cuts on the inside and outside of the arm would occur in opposite directions. Since burial 17 had multiple cuts on the inside and outside of the humerus in the same direction, expert counsel was sought.

The late Dr. William Maples (see Maples and Browning 1994), a University of

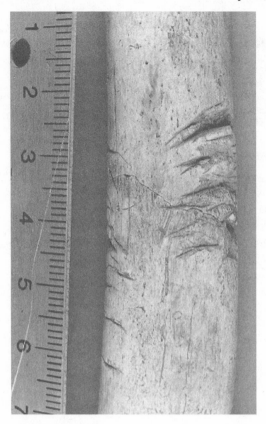

8. Close-up view of tiger shark tooth marks on lateral and posterior surface of humeral shaft. Photo by Peter E. Siegel (used by permission).

Florida forensic anthropologist, examined detailed photographs provided by Siegel. He was not told where the bone came from, or any other information about its context (although he knew that we worked in the West Indies). His first suggestion was that a machete caused the cuts. I explained that there were no metal tools available at the time the wound was made. Next he suggested obsidian, but again there are no obsidian tools from this area. He stated that a chert (flint) tool might be possible, but that it was difficult to sharpen stone tools to the point at which they could produce such sharp cuts. Moreover, he noted that there were multiple cuts in close proximity that were all in the same direction. These were not the wounds a living individual would get, for example, in an axe or machete fight. If this individual was fending off attack then the multiple cuts would have been widely spaced on the humerus and lower arm. Moreover, defensive wounds are far more common on the forearm (we naturally raise our arm in front of us to fend off attack) than on the upper arm. If the cut marks were caused by human agency, they would have had to

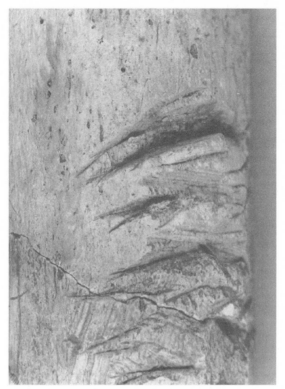

9. Extreme close-up of the damage. Note the horizontal rows of microcuts that resulted from the serrations on the tiger shark's teeth. Photo by Peter E. Siegel (used by permission).

occur after the individual was incapacitated. The key, however, was the tiny striations associated with the cuts. These are not typical of human tools. When asked whether a shark could have produced such cut marks, he exclaimed, "Absolutely." He directed me to George Burgess, keeper of the International Shark Attack File, which he maintains in conjunction with the American Elasmobranch Society.

Burgess has reviewed more than three thousand cases of shark attacks on humans. After examining the photographs, Burgess concluded that the markings were typical of bone damage inflicted by a shark. Moreover, he felt that the striations associated with the cuts made it likely that the culprit was a tiger shark. He reported that the tiger shark will bite its victim, and if it is not able to sever the appendage on its first bite it will tear the flesh and bite again, all the while twisting its body to use its weight and strength as leverage. Often, the appendage will be severed at a joint. This is exactly what we see with burial 17. Apparently the shark was not able to bite through the humerus on its first try. It must have released its bite, bit again, and tore the arm off at the elbow.

For us, life is composed of a series of individual events, yet the most an archaeologist usually can hope to achieve is generalizations about what happened in the past. In certain rare instances, such as this man from Maisabel, we see life and death frozen in an instant. Just when you thought it was safe to go back into the water.

5
The Age of Reptiles

On land I saw no animal of any kind except parrots and lizards.

—Christopher Columbus, 1492

The name iguana (*higuana*) is a Taíno word. The syllable *gua* begins the Taíno words for gold, parrot, fire, and the names of many caciques. It is possible that *gua* was a designation for a favored thing, although Granberry and Vescelius translate *gua* as "our." Indeed, iguanas were one of the favored foods of the Taínos, but by the time the Spanish arrived, iguanas were so rare they were reserved only for the caciques.

This situation suited the Spanish just fine. The Spanish considered iguanas to be extremely ugly beasts that were not suited for human consumption. While sailing along the south coast of Cuba on his second voyage, Columbus entered the harbor at Guantanámo Bay and met a group of fishermen who were smoking fish and iguanas in preparation for a feast that their cacique was planning to host. The Spanish helped themselves to the smoked fish, but left the iguanas. The Taínos expressed great satisfaction that the iguanas were not eaten because they were a highly prized food that was difficult to find. Today on the Guantanámo Bay U.S. Naval Base, terrestrial animals such as iguanas and a large rat called a hutia are extremely common as they no longer have any human predators inside the base boundaries (see plate 6).

By the time Gonzalo Fernández de Oviedo wrote his natural history of the Caribbean islands (first published in 1526), at least a few of the Spanish had come around to the delicacies of these islands, for he reports "the animal [iguana] is better to eat than to see" and describes the flesh "as good or better than rabbit." He

TAÍNO WORD	TRANSLATION
Higuana	Iguana
Caguaya	Common lizard
Guey	Sun
Anoli	Anole lizard
Ameiva	Skink
Bayoya	Curlytail lizard
Maja	Large snake (boa)
Jujo	Small snake

further describes the Taíno keeping the iguanas tied or penned up in their villages, stating that they could survive up to twenty days without food or water, or longer if they were fed cassava bread, which they apparently appreciated.

Another distinction given the iguana was the special way they were prepared before cooking. Peter Martyr D'Anghera, another of the early Spanish chroniclers, reported: "as a distinction from other game, they removed the entrails from iguanas." He described the preferred Taíno method of cooking the animal as boiling it in a large pot heavily seasoned with hot pepper until, after a time, "from the interior of the iguana exuded a savoury stew."

There are several genera and a number of species of iguanas that were once common in the Caribbean Islands. The rock iguanas of the Greater Antilles and the Bahama archipelago are a ground-dwelling species. The smallest species of all the rock iguanas still survives on the small cays of the Turks & Caicos Islands. Today, they reach an average length of fifty centimeters (twenty inches) in body length (including the tail). However, they were not always so small. When the first Taínos reached Grand Turk about thirteen hundred years ago, they found themselves in something of a Jurassic Park. Approaching the beach in their canoes, they came upon the tracks of large green turtles who had just laid their eggs, saw large iguanas sunning themselves on the sand, and must have been curious about the massive tortoises (now extinct) plodding slowly through the bush.

This was the Age of Reptiles for Grand Turk. No humans—and for that matter, no mammals—were present on the island and these reptilian creatures grew large due to a lack of predators. Iguana bones from the archaeological site of Coralie, which dates to the initial human colonization of the island (see chapter 22), revealed that Grand Turk iguanas were once more than three feet long! This is the size of iguanas found on Hispaniola and Cuba.

Yet within four hundred years, the nesting turtles, tortoises, and iguanas had

10. Picnic Area at Guantanámo Naval Base reminding people not to feed the iguanas (or barbeque them). Photo by Lisabeth A. Carlson.

been driven to extinction on most islands. They were meat for the hungry humans who were spreading through the islands. We are fortunate that iguanas still survive in a few isolated locations in the Caribbean. Green turtles no longer nest on many of these islands and the giant tortoises have been gone so long that there is no collective memory of them ever having been in the West Indies at all.

The general term the Taíno used for lizards was *caguaya*. Embedded in this word is the Taíno term for sun (*guey*), and perhaps this common term for all lizards describes the action of sunning themselves that is peculiar to these reptiles.

The Taíno words *anoli* and *ameiva* are not in common use today, but they are the scientific genus names for the primary lizard species in the West Indies. The distinctive curly tail lizards (*bayoya*) still inhabit the bush on many Lucayan Islands. Their bones are found in numerous archaeological sites where they may represent a small

11. Rock iguana bones. The top row comes from a typically sized specimen, while the bottom row comes from the iguanas excavated at the Coralie site on Grand Turk. The same bone elements are shown in each row. Scale is in centimeters. Photo by Lisabeth A. Carlson.

package of meat added to the pepper pot, even though these creatures would contribute little to the food supply. It is also possible that small lizards are natural, not cultural, additions to these sites. The capture of lizards for pets by children is worth considering; today a children's game involves capturing anoles, allowing them to bite one's earlobe, and wearing them as living lizard earrings!

Lizards held a special place in the belief system of the Taínos. According to their origin myth, an individual named *Macoel* was the ever-vigilant nocturnal guardian of the cave from which the first Taínos emerged. He was a reptile who sat motionless and camouflaged against the cave rock walls. The name Macoel means "he of the eyes that do not blink," and indeed, lizards have eyes that do not appear to close. Macoel, as the story goes, was turned to stone by the sun one evening for shirking his duties. Occasionally, the Taínos carved petroglyphs of lizards on the entrances of caves to symbolize Macoel. Another reptile representation focuses on the set of scales on the forehead of the lizard that appears to be an eye, a third all-seeing eye. This "saurian pineal" is viewed by some as the origin of the Cyclops, the mythical being with one unblinking eye in the middle of its forehead.

Snakes are the only other terrestrial reptiles in the Lucayan Islands. The most common species are boas: pygmy boas that reach a maximum length of about thirty centimeters (twelve inches) and other boas that can grow to one and one-half meters (five feet) in length.

Columbus and the Spanish chroniclers did not say much about the snakes of the New World except to point out that they typically were not poisonous. This fact is one of the many great things about doing archaeological research in the Caribbean. There are, however, exceptions. The central zone of the island of St. Lucia is home to extremely venomous "fer de lance." We saw a surprising number of people in this area with useless arms and legs who had been bitten by this snake whose venom attacks the central nervous system. In Trinidad, we encountered the deadly "mapapee," and one of our crew spent several days in the hospital after being bit by a very small snake. Yet these isolated populations pale in comparison to archaeological research in Florida where there are many deadly snakes, and snake boots and snakebite kits are common field gear.

The Spanish recorded several Taíno names for snakes. The term *maja* may have been used in reference to the large boa constrictors found in the Greater Antilles. *Ma* is an adjective that means "big." *Ja* was the sound the Taíno made in awe or admiration of something. (In our language, something akin to the word "wow!"). So the Taíno word for boa constrictors roughly translates as "big wow." The Spanish described some very large snakes on the island of Hispaniola—"20 feet long and thicker than a man's fist." As far as we now know, there never were any snakes worthy of the term *maja* on the Lucayan Islands.

One of the basic principles of island biogeography is that small islands tend to support animals that are either unusually large or unusually small—basically giants or dwarfs. This is because of the coexisting factors of a lack of predators and a limited amount of space and food. One of the smallest boas in the world is found in the Turks & Caicos Islands. The Taíno word for small snake was *jujo*. Unfortunately, unscrupulous collectors have captured these harmless snakes for sale in pet shops. Several years ago we heard of a collector who paid local children on Middle and North Caicos fifty cents per snake, and then sold them in the United States for hundreds of dollars each.

Like all people, the Taínos were keen observers of the natural world that surrounded them. Although they exploited many of these species for food, they also recognized the unique creatures that shared their world. In some cases associating them with mythical beings highlighted the qualities of these animals. Many things have changed since the arrival of humans, and much of it has been to the detriment of the local fauna. Yet by recognizing the uniqueness of these islands, we may be able to save many of the species that the Taínos and we have come to know and love.

6
Catch of the Day

Here the fishes are so unlike ours that it is amazing; there are some like dorados, of the brightest colors in the world—blue, yellow, red, multi-colored, colored in a thousand ways; and the colors so bright that anyone would marvel and take a great delight in seeing them.

—Christopher Columbus, October 17, 1492

The islands of the Bahama archipelago are truly blessed. The crystal clear waters surrounding the islands contain an abundance of marine life. As Columbus noted, many of these are marvelous to see, while others are marvelous to eat. The Spanish recorded more than sixty Taíno names for fishes, sharks, and marine mammals. Several of the names such as manatee (*manati*) and barracuda (*baracutey*) are in common use today.

There is a tendency to think that peoples in the past consumed foods simply to satisfy their hunger. Yet, every culture in the world has developed its own unique cuisine. Unfortunately, the Spanish did not record any Taíno recipes. Nevertheless, we know that the Taínos grilled, barbecued, smoked, salted, and stewed fish with vegetables and chili peppers. They may also have baked fish in stone-lined pits (much like the modern clam bake), and fried fish on flat clay griddles. Fish was the mainstay of the Taíno diet. In fact, one might wonder how many children complained to their mothers: "Grouper for dinner, again?"

Taíno meals were not as one dimensional as we might expect. At the Coralie site on the north end of Grand Turk, we excavated the remains of meals that were prepared in an overturned carapace of a sea turtle, which included fishes and iguanas in addition to turtle meat.

The Spanish noted that the most common Taíno fishing techniques used hook and line, basket traps, nets, and weirs. With regard to weirs, older residents of Middle Caicos told us that Farm Creek Pond (near Bambarra) once had a natural

TAÍNO WORD	TRANSLATION
Manati	Manatee
Baracutey	Barracuda
Bonasí	Black grouper
Guajil	Yellowfin grouper
Jocú	Dog snapper
Pargo	Snapper or red snapper
Caji	Schoolmaster snapper
Chibí	Bar jack
Guaymen	Yellow jack
Buyón	Parrotfish (large and esteemed), likely stoplight
Cachicata	Grunt
Jallao	Margate (large grunt)

barrier (a sandbar) across its mouth, and that during periods of extreme low tide you could walk out on the dry lakebed and pick up fish by hand. Today, this pond is entirely landlocked. In similar ponds and shallow bays, the Taínos kept fish in corrals of interwoven branches or canes. In this way the fishes were kept alive until they were needed as food.

Archaeologists are able to identify many of the fishes consumed in pre-Columbian sites using a comparative method that is known as zooarchaeology. Zooarchaeologists carefully collect samples of animal bones from archaeological sites and then identify them by comparing the bones to known species. Using this approach we now know that the most common fishes in West Indian archaeological deposits were grunts, parrotfishes, groupers, snappers, and jacks. The Spanish recorded Taíno names for many different species within these common fish families (see chapter 9).

The most common food fish at the site of MC-6 on Middle Caicos was bonefish. This is due to the location of this site, which is on the southern bank-side shore of the island. Flats fishes were readily available close by the site, unlike reef fishes. Today, catching bonefish is a popular activity among sport fishermen and women, yet very few people consider eating them. However, their flesh is firm and flakey between all those small bones. Unlike today, "boniness" was not a criterion in prehistoric times for determining the palatability of various fish species.

Flesh preferences are often culturally defined. Looking at archaeological sites throughout the Lucayan Islands, the Taínos' favorite fish appears to be parrotfish and grunts. Is this because they couldn't as easily capture the "better tasting" snappers or groupers? Were these high-quality resources overfished, necessitating the focus on lower-quality fish? Is it possible they really preferred these fish species? Parrotfish are a soft-fleshed but flavorful fish that is not esteemed in modern fish markets primarily because the flesh tends to spoil quickly. This would not have been a factor in prehistoric times. Grunts have tasty, firm white flesh that is perfect for smoking. Grunts and parrotfish are the most common fishes on the near-shore reefs.

One deterrent to fish edibility that affects both prehistoric and modern peoples is the possibility of ciguatera poisoning. This occurs most famously in barracuda but is also common in jacks, groupers, and snappers, as these are all high-trophic-level carnivores. Jacks can be very common in archaeological sites, but by modern standards they are considered barely edible. Snappers and groupers have the gold standard of fish flesh—firm, mild, "meaty" flesh that is low in fat and contains few bones. The Taíno diet always included these carnivore fishes but they were never the dominant fish that they are in today's modern diet.

When Taíno men came home from the sea they knew exactly what types of fish they were eating, and their wives would prepare the fish in appropriate dishes. Today, zooarchaeologists usually know which fish they are eating based on years of studying bones (and years of enjoying Caribbean seafood). In recent years the demand for seafood has resulted in the importation of foreign species that mimic, but fail to meet, the qualities of our most popular fishes. In fact, it recently was reported that 80 percent of the seafood consumed in the United States was imported from a foreign country. You can no longer be certain what you are served, which raises the question: Do you know which fish you are eating?

Following Columbus's first voyage there was a huge exchange of foods between the Americas and Europe. This "Columbian Exchange" sent mostly plant foods such as corn, beans, squash, tomatoes, potatoes, vanilla, and chocolate to Europe; with cattle, goats, sheep, pigs, wheat, olives, and various other domesticates to the Americas. We are in the midst of what might be called the Asian Exchange. In order to meet increasing demand for certain fishes, in the face of declining stocks due to overfishing, tons of fish are imported from Asia every year. The problem that has developed is that these fish often are mislabeled as grouper or other prized food fishes. In some ways this situation is reminiscent of the shift from American lobster to the less expensive Caribbean spiny lobster in U.S. restaurants over the past three decades. The two are not the same; they taste different and have different flesh textures, yet both are marketed as "lobster."

The present situation is more extreme. The Florida attorney general's office recently tested twenty-four grouper samples from Florida restaurants and only seven of the twenty-four were confirmed grouper. A common substitute is Asian catfish. Their suppliers either duped the restaurateurs or the restaurants were complicit in turning a blind eye to what they must have known was not really grouper. To counter this trend of misrepresentation the Florida Department of Agriculture recently posted a web page to help consumers distinguish Florida grouper from Asian catfish: http://www.fl-seafood.com/consumers/grouper_substitution.htm.

So how do you know if the fish that you were served is the same as advertised? If you are in the West Indies and you are eating at a local restaurant you can relax (although the cruise ships are provisioned in Florida so there could be some problems there). You could ask your waiter if the grouper is from the genus *Epinephelus* or if the red snapper is *Lutjanus,* and then watch his startled response. You can send a portion of your meal for DNA testing, but this will add considerably to the cost of the meal. Actually, if you order a grouper sandwich smothered in tartar sauce or a grouper filet covered in Creole or pepper sauce (a more Taíno way of dining), then it doesn't really matter what kind of fish you are eating, and it is virtually impossible to tell.

We can offer you another solution, but it requires ordering the whole fish and then checking its teeth. Groupers have hundreds of tiny pointed teeth that curve up the inside of the mouth. Snappers' teeth lie only on one plane and they have large canines at the front. Parrotfish teeth can't be mistaken for any other fish as they have plates with multiple rows of diamond shaped teeth (they tend to lose a lot of teeth biting coral heads) (see plates 7 and 8). Grunts and jacks both have a single row of small teeth. Barracuda have razor-sharp flat teeth with sharp points that are similar to the teeth of large tunas. Their large, flat teeth were commonly worked into pendants. These differences in anatomy reflect different fish diets, with the carnivorous fish having the sharp pointed teeth and the herbivores having teeth for crushing and grinding.

To us, the best solution is to eat like a Taíno. You can go fishing and capture your dinner with total confidence in the species you are eating. You can go to the priciest of restaurants and trust to their honesty. Or you can avoid grouper and snapper and order fish like parrotfish, grunt, and porgy. You won't find these at upscale restaurants, but there are many local establishments that know how to prepare these in delicious dishes. While recently dining in Port Royal, Jamaica, a group of us or-

12. The Taíno word *baracutey* described the fish we today call barracuda, but it was also a term for being solitary, as in a person or animal that traveled alone. Photo by Barbara Shively (used by permission).

13. The barracuda is a dangerous predator that has numerous razor-sharp pointed teeth. Photo by Lisabeth A. Carlson.

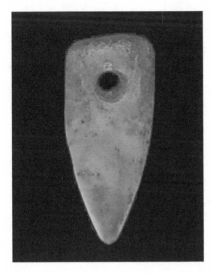

14. Drilled barracuda tooth pendant. Excavated from Site AR-39 (Río Tanamá Site 2) in Puerto Rico. Photo by Lisabeth A. Carlson. Artifacts reproduced by permission of the U.S. Army Corps of Engineers, Jacksonville District.

dered the "steamed fish." When you inquire about what kind of fish you will be served in these small fishing villages the answer is often "reef fish." Each person at the table that night got a different species of reef fish, among them grunts, parrotfish, and juvenile groupers. Each was tasty and prepared well and we definitely knew what we were eating. Now add a little pepper sauce, and you will recognize immediately the fabulous flavor of Taíno dining.

7
Birdland

The flocks of parrots that darken the sun and the large and small birds of so many species are so different from our own that it is a wonder. In addition, there are trees of a thousand kinds, all with fruit according to their kind, and they all give off a marvelous fragrance. I am the saddest man in the world for not knowing what kind of things these are because I am very sure that they are valuable.

—Christopher Columbus, October 21, 1492
(Crooked Island, The Bahamas)

The Taínos kept parrots, traded them and their feathers widely, and gave them to the Spanish as gifts. Upon Columbus's first landing in the New World, the Lucayan Indians presented him with a parrot. Three years later, Columbus shipped sixty of the birds to Spain. Nowadays, more than five hundred years later, the skies are no longer darkened by flocks of parrots. In fact, if you want to see even a few of the bright green and red Cuban parrots in The Bahamas you have to go to either Great Inagua or Abaco, the only two islands where they survive. Native parrots survive today on other Caribbean islands, but in most places they are threatened or endangered.

For many other kinds of birds, however, their disappearance from Caribbean islands took place well before the arrival of Europeans. As early as 1526 Oviedo commented, "Nowhere have I seen fewer birds than on that island." He was referring to Hispaniola, which was called *Ayiti* (Haiti) by the Taíno.

Most people know the story of the canary in the coal mine. The use of these birds to tell whether or not the air was safe to breathe is mirrored in the presence and absence of birds from archaeological deposits. Many native bird populations were decimated soon after humans first arrived on Pacific and Caribbean islands, typically one to several thousand years ago. Human-induced extinctions are not just the outcome of modern development or European colonization; the local extirpation of many animals, especially birds, began with the initial arrival of people in these tropical island settings.

Our colleague and coauthor of this chapter, Dr. David Steadman (curator of Ornithology at the Florida Museum of Natural History), has shown that the native

TAÍNO WORD	TRANSLATION
Ayiti	Hispaniola/Española; source of word "Haiti"
Mucaro	Owl or night bird
Guaraguao	Hawk
Guincho	Falcon
Yegua	Rail
Bajani	Dove
Aon	Dog
Arcabuca	Forest
Sabana	Savannah

bird populations were severely decimated soon after humans first arrived on Pacific and Caribbean islands (Steadman 2006). Steadman recently has been studying animal bones from Indian Cave on Middle Caicos. This cavern has a fantastic record of prehistoric life preserved in sediments more than two meters deep. Many of the fossil bones in these deposits are from birds and other small animals (lizards, snakes, bats)—the remnants of meals from owls (*mucaro*) that lived in the cavern over thousands of years. To date, Steadman has identified the bones of fifty species of birds from Indian Cave, including twenty-seven that are no longer found on Middle Caicos or, in most cases, anywhere else in the Turks & Caicos Islands. They include such diverse types of birds as petrels, geese, hawks (*guaraguao*), eagles, falcons (*guincho*), rails (*yegua*), pigeons, parrots, owls, hummingbirds, and swallows.

Islands, especially small islands, tend to have very fragile ecosystems (see Quamman 1996). Many of the birds that disappear from an island after people arrive are extirpated indirectly by human modifications to the landscape. The Taínos cleared forests for their villages and gardens and to obtain building materials.

The Taínos also introduced species of plants and animals that were not native to the region. They hunted with the help of small dogs that they called *aon*. The impacts of dogs during Taíno times and after, the rats and cats and pigs brought by the Spanish and, more recently, the mongoose have had devastating effects on local animals who were not accustomed to these predators. The mongoose, for example, found that native birds, lizards, and snakes were far easier prey than the rats and poisonous snakes they were introduced to control. Oviedo noted that a large number of dogs and cats that were brought to these islands from Spain ended up feral and "quite vicious, especially the dogs."

The Coralie site on Grand Turk was a camp where sea turtles, tortoises, iguanas, and fishes were captured and prepared, perhaps mostly for export to Haiti (see chapter 22). Even this low-density settlement had a profound impact on the ecology of the island.

About half of the twenty or so species of birds identified at the Coralie site are no longer found on Grand Turk. The fact that bones from two species of parrots were found on both Grand Turk and Middle Caicos coincides with the botanical evidence that these islands were more heavily wooded in the past, supporting what the Taínos called *arcabuco* (forests). In the latest deposits in the Coralie site (after AD 1000) no remains from birds inhabiting wooded habitats were found, suggesting that the forests were replaced, likely through slash-and-burn agricultural techniques, by a dry scrub or grassland (called *sabana* by the Taíno). An unusual, rare bird called the thick-knee was identified only in the late post–AD 1000 deposits. This bird is found on just one island in the Caribbean today—Hispaniola, where it barely survives in dry habitats.

Changing landscapes and new predators were not the only causes of local extinctions. Some species of birds may have been driven to extinction by overhunting. The first inhabitants of Grand Turk had a readily available and constant supply of bird meat and eggs, although the resources were not inexhaustible. Looking at bones from the Coralie site, it seems that some of the Taíno's favorite meals were provided by ducks, particularly the West Indian whistling duck, and two species of boobies—the red-footed booby and the masked booby. Boobies are large-bodied birds that build nests on the ground and form large colonies during nesting season. A single bird could provide between one and two kilograms of meat (two to five pounds). According to Oviedo, boobies would sometimes fly out to Spanish ships and rest on the yards and masts: "The birds are so stupid and remain there so long that they are easily captured by hand. For this reason the sailors call them 'boobies.'" (The name booby is derived from the Spanish "bobo," which means clown or fool.) Oviedo also commented, "they are not good to eat, but sailors do eat them sometimes."

The Taínos ate them also. During the nesting season they were easily captured on the ground. Apparently until about one thousand years ago, colonies of both masked and red-footed boobies nested on Grand Turk. Boobies do not nest or reside in the waters of the Turks & Caicos today, although the masked booby still inhabits some of The Bahamas. Whistling ducks are still found locally in the Caicos, but not in the Turks Islands.

After the Taíno's favorite species of birds got harder to find on Grand Turk, the most common bird bones recovered at the Coralie site became pigeons, doves (*bajani*), and crows. Crows are still ubiquitous today; nearly everywhere we have worked in these islands, Cuban crows were continually squawking.

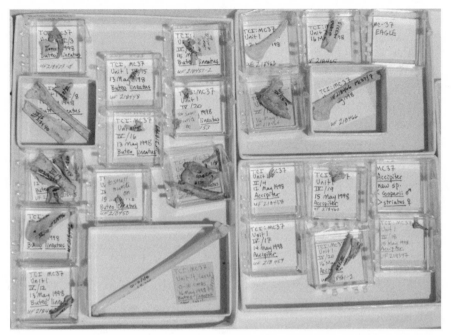

15. These bones found in excavations of Indian Cave, Middle Caicos, are from both living and extinct species of birds. Photo by David W. Steadman (used by permission).

Birds are also important to archaeologists because some can tell us about the season when a site was occupied. For example, Steadman identified two winter residents, the lesser scaup and ring-billed gull, in the faunal samples from MC-6 on Middle Caicos. The presence of these bird bones, the remnants of meals, indicates that the site was occupied during the winter.

Today the most important bird in the islands is the chicken. Having stayed in places where roosters were being raised for cockfights, the constant racket of each bird trying to out-crow the next is enough to make you wish they were never imported. Chickens, which are native to Southeast Asia, were brought to Europe during the ninth century. Although they are not listed in the manifests from Columbus's earliest voyages, they were identified in the archaeological deposits of La Isabela, the first European New World colony, founded in 1493 on the north coast of what is now the Dominican Republic.

No chickens have been found at the site of En Bas Saline in Haiti, excavated by our colleague Dr. Kathleen Deagan of the Florida Museum of Natural History. En Bas Saline is thought to be the site of La Navidad, Columbus's doomed 1492 fort housing the survivors of the shipwrecked *Santa María*. At the later site of Puerto Real in Haiti (founded in 1503), chickens and pigs were the most common animals recovered in the archaeological deposits. Oviedo did note that although Hispaniola had few native birds, "there are many Spanish hens and good capons."

If the chicken did not exist in the New World until 1493, this naturally begs the question: What did other bird meats taste like? It is probably safe to say that many of us have never eaten pigeons or doves, much less parrots or owls. To the Taíno, however, nearly all species of native birds were potential culinary treats. Even crows, as well as "fishy" birds, such as shearwaters, boobies, herons, flamingos, and terns, were eaten when available.

As one species after another declined or disappeared, the Taíno diet became less varied with time. And just as Columbus was saddened by not knowing the local species and their value, we are saddened that birdland now exists mostly as the skeletal remains housed in museum collections.

8
Gone Fishin'

Give a man a fish, and he'll eat for a day. Teach a man to fish, and he'll sit in a boat drinking beer all day.

—Anonymous

Fishing is a social experience. Even if you don't fish with other people, some part of your day fishing will involve socializing. In our culture we have the bar at the marina, but every culture has some form of this. When working at an archaeological site on a tiny island off the north coast of Haiti, a stream of Haitian fishing sloops visited us each afternoon. The fishermen would tie up to the dock, build a lean-to to shield themselves from the sun, and hang out. They ate, drank, went to the bathroom on the island, smoked, and told stories. So a day of fishing was really a morning of fishing and an afternoon of being with friends. This was sufficient to make a living even in the over-fished waters of present-day Haiti. Imagine the ease of feeding oneself in an environment with a natural abundance of resources, such as the landscape of the prehistoric Lucayan Islands.

You can imagine the Taíno Indians fishing in much this same way. Women were often responsible for horticulture, gathering shellfish and wild plants, and preparing meals. Fishing was likely the major male activity in this culture. Men fished and, we can hypothesize, socialized.

Fish were a symbol of life and nourishment in Taíno mythology and the most important animal food to the Taínos. The Taíno mostly fished in waters on the lee side of islands and off small cays. This is also where most of the archaeological sites are located.

Reconstructing the behaviors of peoples who lived in the past requires a complicated sequence of logic and inference. (This is why archaeologists spend more

TAÍNO WORD	TRANSLATION
Baira	Bow (of a bow and arrow)
Cabuya	Fishing line
Jico (or *Hico*)	Rope/cord to hang hammock
Carobei (or *Sarobey*)	Cotton
Henequen	Sisal
Potala	Stone net weight
Guaicán or *Pez reverso*	Remora

years in college than do medical doctors!) On the one hand, we often possess written descriptions of activities that were practiced when Europeans arrived on the scene, along with the names of particular animals that were of importance to those making these written records. On the other, we have archaeological materials that include various tools that have been preserved and the bones of animals that have survived hundreds of years of burial in archaeological sites. There are numerous problems with assigning a particular use to a particular object (which often requires an analysis of form as well as use-wear evidence). Moreover, our samples are only subsets of the range of materials that were used in the past. For example, large conch shells were typically discarded on the beach so the number, size, and characteristics of the conch shells excavated in a site will not reflect the full range of conch use. In sum, we are left trying to piece together puzzles in which many of the pieces are missing.

Bartolomé de las Casas reported that the Lucayan Islanders used bow and arrow to capture fish. The Taíno word for bow was *baira*. This technique was well adapted to the calm, clear waters of these islands. It is likely that spears were used in the same way. There is also evidence for the use of hook and line. Several fishhooks made from the whelk (West Indian top shell) were recovered from the Anse à la Gourde site in Guadeloupe, and a single broken specimen was excavated from the MC-6 site on Middle Caicos. Wooden fishhooks have been recovered from a cave site on Crooked Island in the Bahamas. If wooden hooks were used, then it is difficult to assess how important this technique was because they are not likely to have survived hundreds of years in the soils of open-air sites. Another clue may be various shells that could have been used as lures or "spinners." For example, modified flamingo tongue snail shells have been recovered from archaeological sites with a rough hole or holes that would facilitate their attachment to a cord. These are often considered jewelry (and called pendants), yet the expedient hole or holes

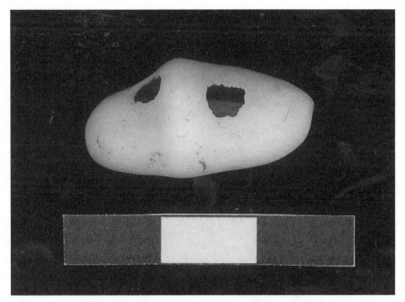

16. Flamingo tongue shell with two rough perforations, possibly used as a fishing lure or line sinker. Excavated from Site Ceiba 11, Puerto Rico. Photo by Lisabeth A. Carlson. Artifacts reproduced by permission of the U.S. Naval Facilities Engineering Command.

indicate that less care was given to making this artifact than was used in making more formal types of personal adornment. Other pieces of shiny (nacreous) shells, including whelks and Caribbean oyster, may also have been used to attract fishes, such as barracuda, to the hook. It is common to find oysters and clam shells roughly perforated, suggesting that these also were used as net or line weights.

Cabuya is the Taíno word for the thin cord used as fishing line made of fibers of the Maguey plant. According to Oviedo, thick cords or ropes used to tie up the Taíno hammocks were called *jico* or *hico* in Taíno. Various kinds of nets made from cotton (*carobei* or *sarobey*) or sisal (*henequen*) were also used to capture fish. Remember that the Taínos' hammocks were in a sense a net.

Most of our evidence for fishing nets comes from the size and kinds of fish identified in archaeological sites. Various size stone and ceramic net weights (*potala*) have been identified in late period sites throughout the Antilles. It has been reported that the Taínos did not use cast nets, but the small size and flat shape of some of these stone weights would be ideal for cast nets. The flat stones provide an aerodynamic surface when the net is cast, and the stones turn vertical to the water's surface on contact, causing the net to sink quickly. Calabashes and light woods

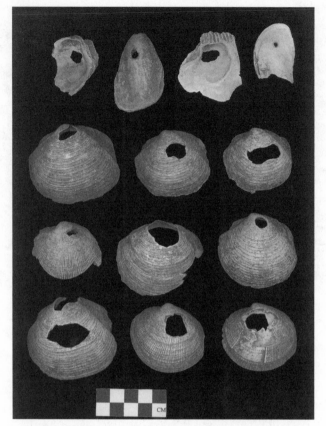

17. Perforated clam and oyster shells (possible net or line sinkers).
Excavated from Site Ceiba 11, Puerto Rico. Photo by Lisabeth A.
Carlson. Artifacts reproduced by permission of the U.S. Naval
Facilities Engineering Command.

likely were used as net floats. In southwest Florida, buttonwood branches were used
as net floats, and large wooden floats were used on turtle nets in the Turks & Caicos
Islands until recently (see plate 9).

The identification of nets and traps often is based on the ecology of the fishes
that were captured. A successful fishing expedition requires the fisherman to "be
the fish." In other words, certain techniques are more effective for catching certain fishes. One of the most common fish in archaeological deposits is the stoplight
parrotfish. This fish is primarily a herbivore that feeds on the algae in coral polyps.
Although these fish can be caught using hook and line, this method would not ac-

18. Notched stone net sinkers (*potala*) excavated from the site of Île à Rat, Haiti. Photo by Lisabeth A. Carlson.

count for the high incidence of these fish, relative to carnivorous fishes, in archaeological deposits. Experiments conducted using Haitian-style basketry traps in the waters around Pine Cay indicated that stoplight parrotfish were the most common species captured and that other herbivorous small fish (such as surgeonfish) that also were common in the site deposits were frequently captured in the traps. The sizes of the fishes in the archaeological samples suggest that traps were being used. The width of the holes in the weave set a minimum size, while the opening sets a maximum size for fishes caught in traps. Fishes in archaeological sites that have sizes restricted to a specific range could be the result of using traps. However, no evidence for the traps themselves has survived.

Oviedo also reported a very unusual form of fishing practiced in Jamaica and Cuba. The Taínos would capture a remora and tie a rope to its tail. The remora has a large suction disk on the top of its head, which it uses to hitch a ride on larger fishes (especially sharks, thus its other common name is "sharksucker") and sea turtles. When the leashed remora attached itself to a large fish or turtle the Taínos would "reel" it in. Oviedo reported the Taíno word for remora was *pez reverso*. In contrast, Hernández Aquino records the term *guaicán*.

Finally, Las Casas also noted that the Taíno kept large groupers in fish corrals and harvested them as needed. Dr. Shaun Sullivan (1981) identified what might have been a fish corral in Farm Creek Pond on Middle Caicos.

Sitting on the beach in Haiti as the local fisherman approached, our thoughts turned to an earlier time when it was Taíno men in dugouts who were returning to the island. Perhaps they even slaked their thirst with a bottle of cassava beer or pineapple wine during their afternoon of socializing. "Drink up, me hearties, yo ho."

9
In the Beginning, God Created Fish

There was a man called Yaya, SPIRIT OF SPIRITS
And no one knew his name.
His son was named Yayael [which means] "Son of Yaya."
This Yayael was banished for wanting to kill his father.
Thus he was banished for four months.
Afterwards his father killed him, put his bones in a gourd,
And hung it from the roof of his house
Where it hung for some time.
It came to pass that one day, desiring to see his son,
Yaya said to his wife, "I want to see our son Yayael."
This made her happy, and taking down the gourd, she turned
It over to see the bones of their son.
From it gushed forth many fishes, big and small.
Seeing that these bones had been turned into fishes,
They decided to eat them.

—Ramón Pané, 1496; translated by
Antonio Stevens-Arroyo (1988)

Fishes were a symbol of life and nourishment in Taíno mythology. They were the most important animal food to the Taínos. Oviedo noted that the Taíno caught "fish that range in size from those smaller than sardines to those so large that two pairs of oxen are necessary to draw them in a cart."

Hernández Aquino (1977), in his dictionary of Taíno words, listed the Taíno's favorite fishes as "*guabina* and *dajado* (freshwater fishes), *robalo* and *pargo* (groupers and snappers), *sabalo* (tarpons), and *moharra* (porgies)." Freshwater fishes are common in archaeological sites in the Greater Antilles, especially at village sites in the interior. Reef fish such as snappers and groupers are found in all coastal sites. These quality fishes were often traded into interior locations. Adult tarpons are not common in West Indian sites, although juveniles are often identified. Porgies are found in small numbers, but were never a staple of the diet.

TAÍNO WORD	TRANSLATION
Grouper Family:	
Robalo	Grouper
Liza	Large grouper
Bonasí	Black grouper
Guajil	Yellowfin grouper
Guaseta/Guasa	Sea bass/grouper
Snapper Family:	
Pargo	Snapper or red snapper
Cachuco	Queen snapper
Cají	Schoolmaster
Jocú	Dog snapper
Muniama	Cardinal snapper
Sesí	Blackfin snapper
Other Fishes:	
Guaymen	Yellow jack
Guabina	Bigmouth sleeper (freshwater)
Guacamaya	Rainbow parrotfish
Buyón ("esteemed")	"Striped parrotfish"; probably stoplight parrotfish
Cachicata	Grunt
Moharra (*Mojarra*)	Striped mojarra; sea bream; porgy
Bajonao	Jolthead porgy

There are five families of fishes that are dietary staples throughout the Lucayan Islands—parrotfish, grunts, groupers, snappers, and jacks. Hernández Aquino lists names for twenty individual species from just these five families (see appendix 1). Many of the Taíno names were later incorporated into the modern scientific names, which help to make the identification of these species possible. *Robalo* and *pargo*, which are very common in archaeological sites, have the most recorded Taíno names.

Several of the species on this list begin with the designation *gua,* including two species of groupers, the rainbow parrotfish, freshwater sleepers, and the yellow jack. Rainbow parrotfish is the largest member of the parrotfish family.

The word *pargo* is the general term for snappers as well as the word for one specific species, red snapper. There also are many recorded individual names for fish in the snapper family. Oviedo noted that the Taíno fished for "broad sardines with red tails . . . which are excellent food and among the best fish found there." This may be a reference to red snapper; however, red snapper is a deep-water fish that is uncommon in archaeological sites. Another broad fish with a red tail is the mahogany snapper, which schools over shallow reefs and would have been one of the more easily captured of the snapper species.

Of the species on the list from Hernández Aquino, schoolmasters are the most common in archaeological sites. The queen snapper seems an unlikely candidate for *cachuco,* since they are caught only below one hundred meters (328 feet). Although the Taínos did fish sometimes in open, deeper waters, the archaeological sites in the Lucayan Islands do not contain evidence of this, probably due to the abundance of fishes on the vast shallow banks. The queen snapper is a fork-tail snapper like the yellowtail. So *cachuco* may have referred to yellowtails, which are common in shallower waters. The *muniama* was identified as a cardinal snapper, another deep-water species.

The two types of fishes found most often in archaeological sites are the stoplight parrotfish and various species of grunts. The only other parrotfish scientific name reported by Hernández Aquino is *Scarus lineolatus,* which is not a known species today. "Lineolatus" means striped, so any striped parrotfish is a candidate for the Taíno name *buyón. Buyón* referred to a species of "esteemed" parrotfish. This most likely refers to the common stoplight parrotfish, because this is a large, plentiful species that may have been esteemed (see plate 8).

The Taíno word for grunt is *cachicata.* Grunts are small fishes that school and can be netted in great numbers. At the Governor's Beach site on Grand Turk and the Clifton site on New Providence Island (The Bahamas), nearly 90 percent of the fish bones collected were from grunts. We know Taíno names for the Spanish grunt and two species of margates. Grunts are ideal for smoking, which would preserve the meat for future consumption and allow for their transport over long distances. It is, perhaps, for this reason that many archaeological sites contain only the head parts of grunts (in other words, the head was removed prior to smoking). Another small fish, *moharra,* are mentioned specifically as a revered and common fish staple, yet they are not common in archaeological site remains. The Taíno word *moharra* has been used in reference to porgies, striped mojarras, and sea breams.

We know of one example where a Taíno adjective that described a type of behavior came to be used as a fish name. The Taíno word *baracutey* meant solitary, as in a person or animal that traveled alone. This accurately describes the fish we today call barracuda.

Because there are so many fishes and so many recorded Taíno names for fishes, and the scientific names for fishes tend to change, deciphering these names is difficult and requires a certain amount of conjecture. The fishes discussed here are a fraction of those recorded. One of the last things we need is more names for fishes, but it is interesting that—like the Eskimos who had many words for the ever-present snow—the Taíno had at least sixty different names for this gift from God.

10
Herbs, Fish, and
Other Scum and Vermin

At a meeting held in 1573 to decide the fate of the colony [St. Augustine, La
Florida], one of the soldiers testified that rations were often short and that
"when there was nothing they ate herbs, fish and other scum and vermin."
—Margaret C. Scarry and Elizabeth J. Reitz, 1990

About 88 percent of the creatures in the sea are animals without backbones—
the invertebrates, which include corals, clams, snails, jellyfish, crabs, and sponges,
among others. As our title indicates, the Spanish were not always enamored of the
local foods that were offered to them by the native peoples. Yet foods that Europeans
once considered unsuited for human consumption are today the choicest morsels
(such as escargot, crab, conch, lobster, calamari, and oysters).

The Taíno Indians collected and consumed vast amounts of these marine creatures as we do today. The most common species preserved in archaeological sites
are crabs, lobsters, conchs, clams, whelks, nerite snails, and chitons. Most of these
items are still on our list of preferred dinner items in the West Indies today, much
the same as it was in the past.

People who live on small islands quickly exhaust their choices of terrestrial foods
such as small mammals, reptiles, and birds. What they are left with is a seemingly
inexhaustible supply of fish and other sea creatures.

Queen conch has been the most important item in the economy of the Lucayan
Islands since people first settled there. Millions of dried conchs were exported from
the Turks & Caicos Islands in the 1960s and 1970s, and the Caicos Conch Farm on
Providenciales is today leading efforts to revive this drastically over-fished resource.
Most Caribbean nations outside of the Bahama archipelago no longer have viable
conch-fishing industries.

The Taíno word for the conch was *cobo,* and they may even have referred specifically to the magnificent queen conch. The sound *ko* translates as outer and *bo*

TAÍNO WORD	TRANSLATION
Cobo	Shell; "outer house"; conch
Bohío	Home
Guamo	Shell trumpet
Juey	Blue land crab
Cocolia	Blue crab, marine
Caguara	Clam (to cut hair)
Donaca	Donax clam

is the word for house (Taínos called their homes *bohío*). So the word *cobo* refers to an animal that carries its house. Conchs (in the islands these snails are pronounced "konk" not "konsch") were a primary food item that was prepared in a variety of ways and was dried and traded between islands. As it is one of the hardest and most plentiful materials in this environment, the Taíno used conch shells as a primary source material for making tools. These included gouges to hollow out canoes, hoes to clear fields for planting, hammers, picks, fishhooks, and net mesh gauges. Conch was fashioned into disk-shaped beads, carved into amulets, and used as inlay materials in more elaborate sculptures.

Conch shells also were fashioned into trumpets. Though queen conchs were made into trumpets, the top-of-the-line variety of trumpets was made from the shell called the Atlantic Triton. These are the largest snails in the Caribbean and their shells can reach a maximum length of forty-five centimeters (eighteen inches). The Taíno had a specific word for trumpets made from this particular shell—*guamo*. Again, the sound *gua* may indicate this was a prized item. Trumpets had everyday uses and the ability to call individuals to action was highly regarded by the Taínos, but they were also important in religious rites. By blowing a shell trumpet, the powers of the spiritual realm were called to action.

The Taíno term for land crab is *juey*. This white soldier crab was a major food item for the Taínos, especially during their initial colonization of the Caribbean islands. Certain archaeological sites were so full of crab remains that archaeologists first called the Indians found in Puerto Rico and the Lesser Antilles the "Crab Culture." Each full-grown male crab can provide up to one pound of meat. The season for hunting land crab is May to October, since they hibernate in the winter. Even so, heavy rains will bring crabs out of their deep burrows in any season (see plate 10).

In archaeological sites primarily it is the claws that are preserved. These claws often show evidence for burning, so roasting crab for dinner was not an uncommon practice. Oviedo specifically noted that crabs were "very good when roasted over coals" and that the Indians were very fond of them. He also noted that if a crab ate poisonous food, such as Manchineel "apples," the crab would not die but its meat would become toxic and could kill the person who ate it!

The other crab that we know the Taíno word for is the blue crab; *cocolia* are marine crabs that live in shallow waters with sandy or muddy bottoms. They are among the few true swimming crabs in the world; their final pair of legs are paddle-shaped "swimmerettes." These crabs are known for biting the toes of unsuspecting waders. Images of crabs have been identified in Taíno art.

Lobsters also are commonly identified in archaeological sites, although the Taíno word for lobster was not recorded. They are recognizable in sites by their mouth-parts, which are very durable because they are used to crush other crustaceans such as crabs. An experimental fishing study conducted by the PRIDE Foundation in the waters surrounding Pine Cay in the Turks & Caicos Islands in 1979 showed that lobster often are caught in the basket traps that modern men and women and Taínos used for fishing.

The Taíno ate many species of clams, but only two words relating to clam were recorded. The first, *caguara*, refers to a specific clam tool. This tool was used to cut hair. Columbus described the very first Indians he encountered upon making landfall in the Bahama archipelago—"Their hair is coarse and short. They wear their hair down over their eyebrows except for a little down the back which they wear long and never cut." Oviedo described some of the Indians of the Greater Antilles as dressing their hair in tufts with shaved areas in between.

In order for them to cut their bangs and shave parts of their head, these clam-shells had to be modified to create a very sharp edge. The Spanish descriptions are not sufficient to identify which clam was used. Tiger lucine clams are very common in archaeological sites, although the Sunrise tellins are also found and have a much thinner and sharper natural edge. Another use of clam shells is as "scrapers," which may have been used to peel root vegetables or scale fish.

The second Taíno word relating to clams is *donaca*. The name has been converted to scientific taxonomy as the genus *Donax*. The tiny donax clams are very common at the water's edge. They were collected by the handfuls along the shoreline and thrown into pepper pots throughout the West Indies. The Indians of the Caribbean and Florida deposited entire middens of the one-inch-long Donax shells. Though they didn't provide much meat, they were easy to collect in vast numbers and were enjoyed by people throughout the circum-Caribbean (see chapter 11).

19. Shell scrapers made from two species of clams. Excavated from the site of Ceiba 11 in eastern Puerto Rico. Photo by Lisabeth A. Carlson. Artifacts reproduced by permission of the U.S. Naval Facilities Engineering Command.

Although the Spanish soldiers who were sent to the New World may have objected to the local fare, complaining that they were reduced to eating "herbs, fish and other scum and vermin," the Taínos and many of the present-day visitors and residents relish these small and tasty morsels from the sea. The Mount Pleasant Guest House on Salt Cay in the Turks & Caicos Islands has been serving up the tastiest "whelk soup" (featuring the West Indian top snail) for decades. A trip to Salt Cay is well worth it for this delicacy alone. Sometimes, good things really do come in small packages!

Plate 1. Saladoid pot stand from Grenada (Florida Museum of Natural History, Wilder Collection). Photo by Lisabeth A. Carlson.

Plate 2. Reconstructed Taíno houses (*caney*) on San Salvador, Bahamas. Photo by William F. Keegan.

Plate 3. Cleared area of stone-lined courtyard at the middle of the site of MC-6 on Middle Caicos. The figures are standing on the two primary stone alignments. Photo by William F. Keegan.

Plate 4. Southern stingray over a reef in the Turks & Caicos Islands. Notice the spine-tipped tail ready to strike. Photo by Barbara Shively (used by permission).

Plate 5. Worked shark teeth from the site of MC-6 on Middle Caicos. Drilled example on right is made from a tiger shark tooth. Tooth on left shows wear from its use as a drill. Photo by Lisabeth A. Carlson.

Plate 6. Large rock iguana on Guantanámo Naval Base. Photo by Lisabeth A. Carlson.

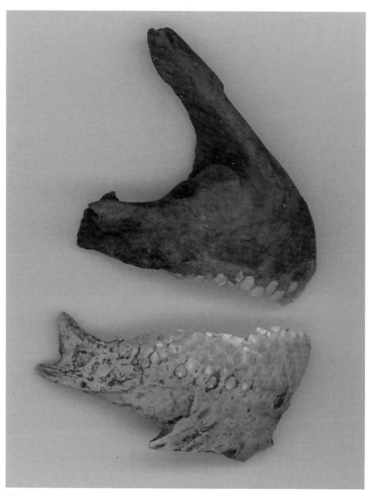

Plate 7. This stoplight parrotfish jawbone is distinctive for its plates of multiple rows of diamond-shaped teeth. Photo by Lisabeth A. Carlson.

Plate 8. The colorful stoplight parrotfish is often the most common fish found in archaeological sites throughout the Lucayan Islands. Photo by Barbara Shively.

Plate 9. Broken ceramic sherds from the site of Île à Rat, Haiti reused as fishing implements. Sherds are notched on two opposing sides so they could be tied to nets or fishing lines. Photo by Lisabeth A. Carlson.

Plate 10. Land crabs (*juey*) for breakfast, Delectable Bay, Acklins Islands, Bahamas. Photo by William F. Keegan.

Plate 11. Chitons and nerites living on rocky intertidal shores. Photo by William F. Keegan.

Plate 12. Whole breadfruits roasting in roadside firepit, Boston Bay, Jamaica. Photo by Lisabeth A. Carlson.

Plate 13. Bougainvillea and Casaurina: Grand Turk's imported landscape. Photo by Corbett McP. Torrence (used by permission).

Plate 14. The tradition of handcrafted boats is best seen in Haiti where types of boats range from dinghys such as this one to sloops up to 35 feet in length. Photo by Lisabeth A. Carlson.

Plate 15. The Taíno word for a flat boat with no keel was *cayuco*. They may have resembled this handmade raft from Haiti. Photo by Lisabeth A. Carlson.

11
The Chip-Chip Gatherers

Chip-chip: a small shellfish found along the tideline of Trinidadian beaches. Gathering chip-chip is a weary task, bringing almost no reward.

—Shiva Naipaul, 1973

In 1973, Shiva Naipaul, the brother of renowned author Sir V. S. Naipaul (Theroux 1998), published the aforementioned book in which he used chip-chip gathering as a metaphor for the futility of life. Chip-chips are tiny *Donax* clams that live in the sand along the tide line and used to be eaten throughout the Caribbean and southeastern United States. They are a delight to watch as they leave the sand with each passing wave, and then burrow furiously back into the sand as the wave ebbs, only to repeat this action with every passing wave.

As Naipaul indicated, gathering and preparing chip-chip is a weary task. Each clam contains less than a gram of meat, and they must be quickly collected between each wave. Because these clams live in sand, their meat must be thoroughly washed after it is removed from the shell. The meat is then grated, which given its small size can be hard on fingertips, and then washed and strained to remove any remaining sand. The effort is worth it. If you are in Trinidad around the time of Carnival (chip-chip is only available in February and March), we strongly recommend that you make every effort to find a place that serves this tasty mollusk.

The consumption of chip-chips has an ancient history. At the St. Catherine site that we excavated in Trinidad there were thousands and thousands of their shells in the midden (refuse) deposit. Although we don't find chip-chip in archaeological sites in the Lucayan Islands, we do find a wide variety of similar small mollusks whose collection and processing provide very small amounts of meat, such as the beaded periwinkles that cling to shoreline rocks. This raises the question, why would anyone endure such a weary task for so little reward? Certainly people had more productive things to do with their time! But this attitude reflects our Western philosophical heritage.

A common assumption, traced back to the writings of Thomas Hobbes (Hobbes 1651), is that life in the past was "nasty, brutish and short." Hobbes' philosophy later received a boost from Thomas Malthus (*An Essay on the Principle of Population,* 1798), who recognized that if population continued to grow unchecked (due to the "unbridled passion of the sexes") that humans would soon outstrip available food resources, resulting in starvation and death. Charles Darwin (*Origin of Species,* 1859) further promoted this conclusion in his oft-quoted notion of "survival of the fittest" (although fitness for Darwin was measured in the contribution of offspring to the next generation).

Alfred Lord Tennyson expressed this view most eloquently in his poem "In Memorium A. H. H." (1849):

Who trusted God was love indeed
And love Creation's final law
Tho' Nature, red in tooth and claw
With ravine, shrieked against his creed.

When the scientific disciplines of evolutionary biology and human ecology first developed, it was assumed that finding enough of the right foods to eat was the main struggle of animals and people (finding an appropriate mate was also important). Given the number of people living today in poverty, the views of Hobbes, Malthus, and Darwin seem not so far-fetched. From this perspective, people reduced to eating tiny clams must surely be on the verge of starvation. After all, a person expends more energy collecting these clams than they get from eating them.

Until the 1970s, notions of progressive cultural evolution viewed modern society as the acme of social development. People in the past must have lived deprived lives and cultures that survived by hunting and gathering were viewed as barely managing to survive. Civilization was only possible with the development of agriculture, which served as the foundation for the world's great civilizations. Then along came Marshall Sahlins (1972), who was one of the first to actually calculate the amount of time hunter-gatherers spent obtaining food. He found that although these people had a paucity of material goods, they spent far less time than modern workers. In sum, they actually worked less hard to meet their needs than most of us do today. For this reason he called them "The Original Affluent Society." Perhaps

H. L. Mencken was right when he said that no laborsaving device has ever saved a minute of labor! (Mencken was the son of a cigar factory owner. Cigars were "invented" by the Taínos, so go ahead and light one up after your next great Caribbean meal.)

Let us reconsider the lowly mollusk. The modern view of eating mollusks is skewed by our notion of superiority over the past. In California the brown land snail is a garden pest, while in France it is escargot. Digging clams in New England and catching scallops in Florida are popular family activities, but most people don't do these to feed their family. Should we really believe that our lifestyle is so different to those who lived in the past?

The consumption of conch by the early inhabitants of the Lucayan Islands seems to make perfect sense. Queen conch provides a large package of meat that is virtually all protein. In addition, if prepared correctly, dried conch can be preserved for up to six months, making this a storable surplus item. But why eat other small snails and clams unless you are starving? Our answer is that the Taínos had the luxury of eating these other mollusks because they were not starving. Like us, they liked them and considered them worth the effort.

Most of the people who visit the Lucayan Islands are primarily interested in the beautiful white sand beaches. We suggest that you take a moment to walk along the rocky shoreline where you will encounter the world of snails and chitons. Covering these rocks you will see thousands of nerites, periwinkles, chitons, and in a few places, the West Indian top shell (whelk). The Taínos ate all of these animals. Close by in the grass flats, there is an array of clams buried among the roots of the turtle grass or mangroves. All you need to do is reach down and pull them up (if they don't "swim" away from your hand). It may be a folly of youth, but a lasting memory from invertebrate zoology class is that the clam's body is folded in half such that its anus and head are side-by-side. It's true; clams defecate on their heads. Yet, clams, oysters, and mussels are considered delicacies (and appetizers) and are fun to gather and cook.

You may be familiar with oysters, mussels, lobsters, and conch, but here are a few delicacies you may not have tried. Chitons are armored creatures that live on the rocks just at the tide line, and they are one of the hardest animals to harvest because the chitons are firmly stuck to the rocks (see plate 11). The local name for them in the Turks & Caicos Islands is "suck rock." A series of eight body plates surround the small, edible body, and these plates are found in the archaeological middens and they are always intact. With no metal tools, the only way the Lucayan Taínos could have harvested these animals without smashing the plates and the meat inside was by using a combination of conch shell tools. The beveled tip of a conch columella would be used to wedge the animal free from the rocks with help from a conch hammer (made from the other spire end of the conch). So is it worth the effort? The resulting small strip of black meat of the chiton is salty, rubbery, and a little slimy. Maybe not.

Another option is the nerite snail. These snails are about an inch in diameter and are easy to pluck off the rocks along the water line. These are best prepared in a soup or stew, which easily releases the muscle from the snail shell. Whelks can be prepared the same way or they can be eaten raw straight off the rocks. This is a larger gastropod that can grow up to four inches in diameter. The shells were modified as tools and ornaments by the Taínos. The meat of the whelk can be picked from the shell with a small pointed tool if you can catch the animal before it slams the door closed. Its "door" is really the stony end of its foot, which fits across the opening of the shell in order to protect its inhabitant. This end is called an "operculum;" they are found in archaeological sites, and some of them are identifiable to the animal they came from. Conchs have a similar hard foot. The way to extract conch meat is to hit a hole in the top spire area and cut the muscle free from the shell with a knife or sharp reed. Modern fishermen and women use machetes to knock a slit in the top of the conch shell. Lucayan Taínos knocked a round hole in the top using the spire of another conch shell.

References to the lowly invertebrates of the world occur in all cultures and from all periods of time. One you may remember comes from an English nursery rhyme:

Mary, Mary quite contrary,
How does your garden grow?
With silver bells and cockle shells
And pretty maids all in a row.

This rhyme has been interpreted as a reference to Mary ("Bloody Mary"), the daughter of Henry VIII. So, what is the subtext of this seemingly innocuous little poem? With the metaphors removed, the poem might read:

Bloody Mary, quite contrary
How does your graveyard grow?
With thumbscrews and genital clamps
And guillotines all in a row.

20. William F. Keegan removing a conch from its shell in the manner of the Taínos. Photo by Lorie Keegan.

Clearly, we have gotten off topic! We started by discussing the seasonal delicacy of chip-chip in Trinidad. For Naipul, clams were a symbol of life's futility; yet for many people, clams and other boneless sea creatures are a source of great joy. Coming back to Hobbes, is it nature that makes life "nasty, brutish and short," or could that be human nature? Let's ask Mary.

12
Eats, Shoots, and Leaves

The Caribbean islands are a great place to take a vacation. One of the most common vacation activities is lying on the beach and reading a good book. In this regard, let us suggest Lynne Truss's (2003) book: *Eats, Shoots, and Leaves.* This runaway bestseller is about, of all things, punctuation. The title comes from a joke about an undereducated nature writer who used the words of the book title to describe the diet of the Panda. The problem is that the punctuation gives the impression that the Panda eats dinner, shoots a gun, and leaves the restaurant (an "Oxford comma" has been added to give the Panda time to escape).

What does that have to do with the Caribbean? First, it places you on the beach reading a good book and it highlights our shift in emphasis from animals to plants. All of our previous chapters have dealt with animals, yet plants were the major component of the Taíno environment, diet, and material culture. Finally, it provides the basis for connecting the seemingly random comments on plants that we offer here.

So you are sitting on the beach reading a good book. The coconut palms and casuarinas are swaying in the breeze. There are banana plants (bananas don't grow on trees) used tastefully as landscaping, and the waiter just brought you a rum-based drink. There are other beautiful flowers—bougainvillea, bird-of-paradise, ginger lilies—blooming in the gardens. But you will not find names for any of these plants in the Taíno dictionary. They were all introduced from other tropical lands. Their presence is the outcome of what Alfred Crosby (1972) called the homogenization of the neo-tropics. There are, however, some intriguing stories.

TAÍNO WORD	TRANSLATION
Mahiz	Corn
Tabaco	Tobacco
Mapu	Large, red tree
Tuna	Prickly pear fruit
unknown	Salt
none	Banana
none	Coconut
none	Sugar
none	Casaurina pine

In this chapter, we will mostly be talking about what is not Taíno. Sometimes you need to define your subject by describing what it isn't. People tend to assume that the environment that surrounds them has always appeared that way. In considering Taíno plants, we begin by describing what came after the Taínos.

In the 1980s there was a television commercial in which a very Navajo-looking woman said, "You call it corn, we call it maize." This statement is inaccurate on many fronts. First, the Navajo use the Aztec word (which was "Xinteotl") for the plant that scientific taxonomy has named *Zea mays*. The word maize actually comes from a Taíno word: *Mahiz* (in Spanish, *maíz*) (pronounced: "my ease"; in contrast to the modern pronunciation: "maze").

The last Native American to call corn "maize" likely died in the sixteenth century. So where did the name "corn" come from? Before the Americas were "discovered," the British used the word "corn" to denote any kind of small bits. This included salt (as in "corned beef") and several cereal plants producing edible seed, such as wheat, rye, oats, or barley. Remember Jack London's (1913) story about John Barleycorn? The Europeans called maize "Indian corn," which was later shortened to just corn. Spanish accounts suggest that *mahiz* was eaten like today as corn-on-the-cob and only rarely was allowed to ripen for the making of cornbread (Johnny-cake). However, recent studies using a microbotanical identification technique called starch-grain analysis indicate that maize was much more important to Taíno subsistence than previously suspected. Corn is often identified on stone tools used for cutting or grinding, which suggests that corn was regularly shredded, dried, and ground into meal.

In his treatise on the Natural History of the New World, Oviedo described a plant with which he was unfamiliar. Because his descriptions were published so early in the exploration of the Americas (1526) many people believed that banana's were native to the Americas. (Note: in order to preserve the pronunciation of a foreign plural name ending in a vowel, it was common, in the past, to insert an apostrophe or tilde; the former has since become known in England as the greengrocer's apostrophe.) Bananas were, in fact, a recent introduction from Southeast Asia.

Coconuts, the plant that typifies the Caribbean landscape, cuisine, and bar tabs, are not native to the Americas. These plants were not Taíno. They were first brought to Europe from the Indian Ocean by the Portuguese in 1499. Rum-based drinks come from sugarcane that the Spanish brought from the Canary Islands in the early sixteenth century. Casuarina pines came from Australia, and most of the flowers here are also on vacation from distant lands.

In an environment where there were so many native fruit trees, it is interesting that the main objective of Captain Bligh's voyage, chronicled in *The Mutiny on the Bounty,* was to bring breadfruit from the Pacific Islands to Jamaica as a way to provide a cheap food source for the slaves. His goals were much the same as those of Sir Walter Raleigh, who, almost two hundred years earlier, brought potatoes from Peru as fodder for the Irish peasants. (Even today in Jamaican markets you need to ask for "Irish.") Captain Bligh failed twice, although he did manage to reach St. Vincent, where a wide variety of Oceanic plants were transplanted in what became the first botanical garden in the West Indies. Breadfruit eventually did reach Jamaica, where it is a staple food today, commonly seen roasting whole in open fires (see plate 12).

The Caribbean islands boast a largely transported, anthropogenic (= human created) landscape (see plate 13). How could this happen? Today the answer is that people willing to spend money to travel to the West Indies have certain expectations concerning what they will find there, and the travel companies that try to convince people to pay for their tours meet these expectations. Similarly, in the past, it had to do with profits. Sugar, indigo, and dyewoods, along with Taíno products—salt, tobacco, and cotton—provided the economic foundation for European expansion in the West Indies. Salt, which was once called "white gold," was a major commodity. Cuban cigars are still considered the finest of tobacco products, and our word tobacco comes from the Taíno word *tabaco.* The Taínos produced, according to las Casas, "a thousand things from cotton," including short skirts for women and belts that had decorative designs created by the addition of shell beads.

The introduction of sugarcane and the cultivation of cotton set in motion the African Diaspora. With the arrival of the Spanish, warfare, excessive demands, mistreatment, and introduced diseases led to the rapid demise of the Taíno peoples. In order to maintain an adequate labor pool the Spanish brought enslaved Africans to the Caribbean and set them to work on sugar and cotton plantations. These are

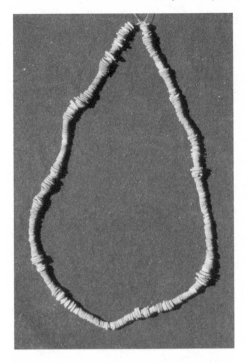

21. Shell bead necklace reconstructed from conch and jewel box shell disk beads excavated at the Governor's Beach site, Grand Turk, where they were manufactured for export. Photo by Corbett McP. Torrence (used by permission).

the ancestors of most of the people who live in the islands today. The mixing of cultures, especially African and Taíno, has created a rich heritage, one based on fishing, farming, medicinal plants, local cuisines, and especially self-reliance. Europeans may have skimmed off the profits, but modern West Indians have persevered.

Deforestation has caused major problems in the islands. Stripped of protective vegetation, the soil becomes baked into a hardpan, and heavy rains can cause incredible floods. In June 2004, severe flooding occurred in southern Haiti and the Dominican Republic. It was reported that the town of Mapou, Haiti, was completely under water. A *New York Times* article used the name Mapou to highlight the ecological devastation that Haitian peoples have wrought on their country. They made special note of the fact that the name Mapou comes from a tree that occupies a special place in the Haitian practice of voodoo. However, there are no longer any mapou trees in Mapou, the implication being that primitive beliefs were belied by the cutting down of sacred trees.

Had the press done more than skim the surface, they would have found deeper meanings. The name for the tree is of Taíno origin (*mapu,* meaning large red tree). It is a very impressive tree that we know firsthand. While in Haiti we were challenged to hike from Labadee to Cap Haitian ("Okap" in Kweyol/Creole). Close to a spring near the top of the mountain overlooking Okap there was a huge tree. It was unlike any tree we had seen in Haiti. It would have taken three people holding hands to encircle its circumference.

How could such a huge tree survive in a country where mango trees (a valuable and imported fruit tree) are felled for lumber? The answer is that the mapou requires a reliable water source, the trunk is usually hollow, there are numerous branches, and cavities in the wood. As a result it does not provide a good source of lumber. It has survived the decimation of Haiti's forests because it is of little value except for shade. The tree achieved a spiritual significance because it grows to an enormous size in a place where most trees are best described as saplings.

All the islands of the West Indies once supported ancient forests of large trees, even the dry Lucayan Islands. In the Turks & Caicos Islands all the trees on Grand Turk, Salt Cay, and South Caicos were cut because they "attracted rain" and thus hindered the production of solar-distilled salt, the major economy of the Turks Islands since the seventeenth century.

The Taínos deserve the last word. It is reported that in an effort to discourage the Spanish invasion of their territory the Taínos fed them the fruit of the prickly pear cactus (*tuna* in Taíno). These fruits apparently can cause a person's urine to turn red when consumed in sufficient quantities. In fact, this cactus fruit was later fed to the chenille worm, which concentrated the red color and was used to produce a dye for clothing. Unfortunately, what may have been a great practical joke (imagine your reaction if your urine suddenly turned red!) was not enough to frighten the Spanish away from Taíno lands. In the end, the Taínos learned the hard way that a Spaniard eats, shoots, and stays.

13
Eat Roots and Leave

The Taínos were an agricultural people. We estimate that they cultivated or managed more than eighty different plants that provided foods, medicines for their ailments, and fibers for nets, rope, and hammocks. Taíno agriculture was not like anything that Europeans had seen before. While the main food crops in Europe were cereal grains, the peoples of the West Indies emphasized root crops. Moreover, European gardens involved plow agriculture where plants were cultivated in neat rows; fields were fertilized with manure from domesticated animals and/or fallowed for a few years in a process of crop rotation. In contrast, Taíno fields must have appeared messy and disorganized.

The Spanish encountered several types of Taíno gardens. First, various plants and herbs requiring special care or of immediate use were planted around houses in what we call "house gardens" (*guada*). These were the precursors of our modern herb and flower gardens, which mainly serve aesthetic purposes. In contrast, Taíno house gardens contained useful species.

The second type of garden was located a short distance away from the main village. Called *conuco*, these were areas of the forest that were cut and burned and then planted in a haphazard manner with a variety of cultigens grown together. Characterized as "slash-and-burn" horticulture, a plot of land was cleared of trees and bushes and then allowed to dry. Large trees were "girdled" to cause them to drop their leaves. Just prior to the start of the next rainy season, the cut vegetation was burned to release nutrients that were bound up in the vegetation. A wide variety of crops were then planted in the cleared-and-burned land, sown with a dig-

TAÍNO WORD	TRANSLATION
Guada	House garden
Conuco	Agricultural field
Coa	Digging stick
Boniata	Sweet potato
Montone	Agricultural mound
Yuca	Manioc
Casabi	Cassava bread
Guayo	Grater board
Cibucán	Basketry tube
Casiripe	Pepper pot
Burén	Ceramic griddle

ging stick (*coa*). A *coa* was about two meters (six feet) long with a fire-hardened tip. They were similar to modern "breaker bars." Given the extreme hardness of clay soils throughout much of the Caribbean, such large heavy tools were essential to cultivate these soils.

The Taíno cultivated multiple varieties of root crops, including many different strains of manioc and sweet potato (*boniata*) along with lesser-known tubers such as arrowroot and yautia or cocoyam. Because these plants matured at different rates, they allowed nearly continuous harvests. The fields remained productive for about four years, after which they were fallowed.

But the tropical forest is what the anthropologist Betty Meggers has called a "counterfeit paradise." By this she means that the lush vegetation belies an impoverished and shallow soil that is susceptible to erosion during heavy rains and is easily baked into a hardpan by the tropical sun. The vegetation must be burned to release the nutrients and fields must be allowed to fallow for decades before new gardens are planted.

It took years for Western agricultural scientists to recognize these unique characteristics of tropical gardens. At first they tried to transform tropical farming into a more regular and orderly system, and for a few years they found good yields from plowed fields, but after that the land was unproductive. They learned the hard way that tropical soils will not support long-term cultivation in the same way as the soils in temperate climates. In the end they had to acknowledge that slash-and-burn techniques were ideally suited to farming in most areas of the tropics.

Still, some soils, particularly those along river flood plains where nutrients were

22. Manioc roots. Photo by William F. Keegan.

annually renewed by flooding, supported a more intensive form of cultivation. In these areas the thin soil layer was piled into semipermanent mounds (*montone*), which provided good drainage and loose soil to plant and harvest root crops. A *montone* was about one meter (three feet) high and three meters (nine feet) in diameter with flat tops.

The Taíno's staple crop was called *yuca,* known today as manioc. The *yuca* was processed into cassava bread called *casabi* by the Taíno. According to Taíno mythology, it was the culture hero *Deminán* and his brothers who stole manioc from the high god *Yaya* and brought it to the Taíno people. The story mirrors other cultures' myths in which humans wrest their means of subsistence from supernatural beings. This myth was referenced and re-created when the Taíno buried stone carvings of *Yocahu* (literally, the giver of manioc) in agricultural fields. The stones were triangular in shape and resembled a sprouting tuber. The god image on the "three-pointed stones" often has an open mouth, which eats the soils to make room for the tubers to grow. *Yocahu* was the Lord of Yuca and also the male fertility god.

Manioc occurs in numerous varieties, but the main distinction is between "bitter" and "sweet." These names refer to the amount of cyanogenic glucosides concentrated in the tissues. Put more directly, all varieties of manioc contain cyanide. The bitter varieties contain toxic levels that require special forms of processing to be edible, while the sweet varieties are less toxic. Sweet manioc can be peeled, cut, and boiled like a potato. By boiling the tuber, the cyanide is released and the flesh becomes edible.

So why grow bitter manioc? Why grow a tuber that is toxic to humans? So toxic, in fact, that the Taíno reportedly used the juice to commit suicide. The answer seems to be that bitter manioc has a higher starch content and can be processed into a flour that can be stored for many months. Sweet manioc is a perishable commodity and must be eaten soon after it is harvested. Manioc is extremely drought resistant, has high calorie content, and can, though it matures in ten months, be stored in the *montone* fields for up to three years before harvesting. Bartolomé de las Casas reported that twenty people working six hours a day for one month to plant manioc in the Taíno fashion could feed three hundred people for two years.

Though manioc is an abundant starch resource, it must be supplemented with fish or other protein sources to provide a healthy diet. This fact was made clear in the late 1960s when the people of the United States were implored to give aid to the starving children of Biafra (Nigeria), whose bellies had grown distended due to a lack of protein in their diet that caused a disease called kwashiorkor. This situation occurred because manioc had been brought from the American tropics to tropical Africa as a way to increase the food supply. The consequences were unanticipated.

During public lectures we often ask members of the audience to raise their hand if they have ever eaten manioc. Very few people do. But when we ask if they have ever eaten tapioca, almost everyone has. Tapioca is made from manioc. A more recent culinary development may also strike a chord. The "fish eggs" at the bottom of the new, haute beverage Bubble Tea is manioc.

The process of transforming the poisonous manioc root into the staple cassava bread begins by peeling the skin away with a sharp implement. Then the flesh was grated to produce a pulp. Grating could have been accomplished in a number of different ways, but one of the most common involves the use of specially prepared grater boards (*guayo*). The boards are made from a flat piece of wood into which small flint chips are embedded and then sealed with the resin from a tree. Moving it across the sharp flakes shreds the tuber. The pulp is then placed in a basket tube (*cibucán*) and squeezed. The *cibucán* is similar to the child's toy known as a Chinese finger puzzle—a woven tube into which you slide your fingers at opposite ends. As you try to pull your fingers out, the tube contracts to hold them fast. By putting the manioc pulp in the *cibucán* and applying pressure to both ends, the tube contracts and extracts the juice from the pulp.

The juice, albeit toxic, was boiled to remove any remaining cyanide and then

23. Ceramic griddle fragments. The examples above show the smooth upper working surface. The unsmoothed exterior surface of the same griddles are shown below. Excavated from Site AR-39 (Río Tanamá Site 2) in Puerto Rico. Photo by Jaime Pagán Jiménez (used by permission). Artifacts reproduced by permission of the U.S. Army Corps of Engineers, Jacksonville District.

used as the base stock for *casiripe* ("pepper pot"). This stew was eaten by using pieces of cassava bread like a spoon.

The manioc pulp was spread out and left to dry. The dried flour would later be spread on a clay griddle (*burén*) over a fire where it was baked into cassava bread. It is the thick sherds of the clay griddles that we find in archaeological sites that provide our best evidence for the baking of cassava bread, although other foods were cooked on these as well. Starch grain analysis on griddles have identified the remains of sweet potato, corn, domesticated beans, and the oils from fish. In addition, charred manioc tubers have been recovered from the Taíno archaeological site of En Bas Saline in Haiti (circa AD 1450).

In 1979, Keegan was excavating an archaeological site on Pine Cay in the Turks & Caicos Islands as part of his master's research. The focus of this research was shell tools made from the Queen conch, and he had purchased manioc from North Caicos to test the efficacy of shell tools for peeling the tubers. The tools worked remarkably well, but only a small fraction of the cassava tubers were used in the experiments. Months later, he returned to Pine Cay with a local resident. Naturally, the first thing they did when they arrived was to look for something to eat.

In those days you couldn't run off to the grocery store. The commissary on Pine Cay was depleted, and the nearest (and only) store was BWI Trading on Providenciales (Provo). Even there supplies were hit or miss. (When Brian Riggs went to Provo to get peanut butter and jelly for Shaun Sullivan's field team on Middle Caicos in 1977, he found only mint jelly in the store. For the next week Sullivan's team had peanut butter and mint jelly sandwiches for lunch.) We peeled, grated, squeezed, and dried the manioc that had been left in the kitchen, and then baked cassava bread. It tasted like cardboard. The bread would have been inedible if it weren't for a can of Hershey's chocolate syrup found left in the cupboard.

Years later, we were returning from a site visit deep in the Haitian countryside. Arriving at the main intersection in the village of Dondon we encountered a woman with five 3-foot-diameter cassava breads balanced on her head. We purchased one for a few Gourds (Haitian currency). It was one of the most delightful snacks we have ever eaten. It was warm and nutty tasting, and had the addictive quality of potato chips or popcorn. Remember this tip: Cassava is best when bought from the head of its baker.

The Spanish immediately recognized the usefulness of manioc. The cassava bread could be stored for long periods, and it came to replace hardtack as the staple for expeditions throughout the Americas. Some Taíno villages were forced to pay tribute in cassava bread, and villages, especially in eastern Hispaniola, were responsible for provisioning Spanish ships. You might say that by providing cassava bread the Taíno could expect that the Spaniards would eat roots and leave.

14
If You Like Piña Coladas . . .

Pineapple and coconut are an interesting combination. While the former comes from the Americas, the latter was introduced from Southeast Asia (via the Canary Islands). The Spanish believed that coconuts had "the most palatable taste of all things one can find on earth." They also really liked pineapples, which they called "piña" because they resembled pinecones. The Taíno called them *anana* or *yayagua*. Here we see the perfect melding of Old and New World fruits (when combined, of course, with rum from Southeast Asian sugarcane and historical American ingenuity in distillation).

When you work in the West Indies it is impossible not to associate your favorite memories with fruits: finding a ripe lime tree near Kew on North Caicos and squeezing its juice into a cold cola after a hot day's work; eating ice cream made from sour sop in Haiti or passion fruit in Puerto Rico; picking a papaya from a trailside tree in the Dominican Republic and, again, drenching it in lime juice fresh from a nearby tree (papaya comes from the Taíno word *ababaia* or *papaya*); walking along in Grenada popping genips and sucking all the sweetness from the fibrous seed, which leaves in your mouth what seems like a wad of chewed newspaper (we were told it would ward off thirst); having pineapple for lunch one afternoon in Haiti, procured and processed with a machete; eating ripe coco plums on West Caicos or sea grapes in Cuba; smelling the freshly picked and cut guava. . . .

Tropical and subtropical fruits are rarely an acquired taste; most of them are sweet and juicy and easy to love at first bite. People in the islands have an advantage because much of the world doesn't have immediate access to these fruits (and

TAÍNO WORD	TRANSLATION
Anana or *Yayagua*	Pineapple
Ababaia or *Papaya*	Papaya
Guanábana	Sour sop
Mamey	Mamey apple
Guayaba	Guava
Caimito	Yellow Sapote
Bija	Achiote
Jagua	Genipap
Guiro	Gourd or Calabash
Yabisi	Fruit or shade tree

when they do, the fruits are usually not ripe when they were picked to ensure that they will make it to market).

Spaniards created an amazing mix of fruits when they arrived in the New World. They brought with them some of the fruits that they had acquired through trade with Africa and Southeast Asia: bitter oranges, sweet oranges, lemons, limes, figs, and dates (although they hadn't yet recognized the importance of citrus in countering scurvy during long ocean voyages). The Taínos, whom they met, had also brought fruit trees with them when they moved from the South American mainland to the islands, and pre-Taíno peoples had previously introduced fruits from Central America to the Greater Antilles. Migrating people tend to not leave home without their favorite plants and animals.

Early Spanish descriptions of the fruits of the Caribbean were glowing in their praise. Pineapples were "one of the best fruits in the world . . . and also very handsome." And, after the pineapple was introduced to North America in the seventeenth century, it was so well received, it became a symbol of hospitality.

Avocado, which West Indians call "pear" (so as not to confuse it with "avocat" or "abocado," which means lawyer in French and Spanish), was reportedly "very good with cheese." The Spanish also noted that the Taíno gave these pear trees no care whatsoever and that God was "the principal gardener." Sour sops (*Guanábana*) were described as "large, cone-shaped fruit, with white, delicate tasting flesh." Actually, they look like spiky green hedgehogs and can reach one foot in length. *Mamey* apples have not been introduced into the North American market yet, but the Spanish thought they tasted "like peaches but better" (can anything really be better than peaches?).

Oviedo made this insightful statement about guavas (*guayaba*): "They have many seeds that are bothersome only to those who eat the fruit for the first time." If you eat them, seeds and all, they are intoxicating. Foods with such a heavenly taste and smell just might be considered sinful. The Taínos associated guavas with the world of the dead. The *opía* or spirits were said to come out at night in the guise of bats and feast on these sweet fruits. The ruler of the world of the dead, *Maquetaurie Guayaba,* has guava as part of his name.

The richness of the fruit trees of the West Indies is in many instances the result of Taíno introductions and management of various tree species. At archaeological sites in Puerto Rico and Hispaniola, Dr. Lee Newsom has studied the contents of Taíno house gardens. She has identified papaya, guava, sour sop, several fruits of the sapotacaea family (star apple, yellow sapote, sapodilla), and panama tree, which is a member of the chocolate family that has edible seeds that can be ground and roasted and made into a beverage. The papaya and panama tree are not native to the West Indies; they were introduced by the ancestors of the Taíno who came from South America, although the homeland of the papaya is Central America. The small, green genip is another South American introduction.

Sapodilla, yellow sapote, and avocado also are originally from Central America and all were introduced to the West Indies before the South American Saladoid migration. Yellow sapote (*Caimito*) is sometimes called "egg fruit" because the flesh has the consistency of a hard-boiled egg yolk. Sapodilla has soft, brown flesh that tastes a bit like root beer. Its bark is the source of chicle, an ingredient of chewing gum. The related species, Star apple, has a green or purple skin and a mucus-like texture.

In the Bahama archipelago, several fruits have been identified in archaeological sites: cocoplum, hog plum, strong bark, and wild lime. Strong bark and wild lime were identified at the Coralie site on Grand Turk. Hog plum grows in clusters of small, yellow fruits with fibrous, juicy pulp and a large seed. The cocoplum grows on windward beaches. Its fruits are dark purple and the size of olives and are much loved by iguanas. Iguanas also love prickly pear, another favorite fruit for the Taínos.

Other types of trees were introduced prehistorically to the islands because their fruits functioned as something other than food. Achiote, originally from lowland South America, has seeds that were ground and made into a bright red dye that the Taínos called *bija*. This red paste was used to color their skin. The color red was associated with Taíno male virility, but *bija* apparently also repelled mosquitoes. Today achiote is used as a natural food coloring that gives us the lovely yellow color in processed American cheese. Cupey was introduced because it was an important source of resin for the Taíno, and Las Casas wrote that the Spanish used it as a substitute for paper.

The genipap seems also to have been introduced from South America. Called *jagua* by the Taíno, the fruit was processed into a black dye and used for tattooing, painting, and possibly for dyeing hair. The Taínos associated the black dye from the *jagua* fruit with representations of the spirit world. The Turks & Caicos National Museum was originally called Genip House after the large genipap tree in the front yard. Fruit trees in the Caribbean are often large trees, and the Taíno word for shade tree is the same as the word for fruit tree (*Yabisi*).

Guiro (calabash and bottle gourd) were among the earliest and most important plants cultivated in the Americas. They were the equivalent of prehispanic canteens and were the main water container among the Lucayan Taínos. The Taínos had no need to make ceramic water bottles because these gourds provided a ready and reliable container.

Europeans were not the first islanders to make alcoholic concoctions from West Indian fruits. "Beer" was made from manioc and maize. The Island Caribs, who lived in the Lesser Antilles, reportedly made a kind of wine from pineapples. So, when in the West Indies, continue in the native tradition. Order a fruit salad made from local fruits; it will taste nothing like the fruits available in other countries. And the next time you combine rum, coconut cream, pineapple juice, lime juice, half-and-half, and ice in a blender, and enjoy a frosty piña colada, remember that you are experiencing the best of both worlds.

15
Boat Trips

Life on an island is just not possible without boats. The history of the Caribbean, both prehistorically and historically, is linked to the ability to build boats and navigate the oceans successfully.

Not just anyone can go out and colonize an isolated, oceanic island. The most important factor is the colonizer's voyaging ability, which is not always linked to how accessible oceanic islands may be to a population. Madagascar lies close to the east coast of Africa but was colonized by people from Indonesia (four thousand miles away!). A similar situation occurs in the Caribbean. It has long been assumed that people entered the Caribbean by island hopping from South America through the steppingstone islands of the Lesser Antilles. Yet present evidence indicates that there were more direct contacts across the Caribbean Sea, and that the Windward Islands of the southern Lesser Antilles were first colonized long after people had settled in Puerto Rico and the Leeward Islands. There is compelling evidence that people from the Isthmo-Colombian area (Colombia, Panama, Costa Rica) were in regular contact with the peoples of the Greater Antilles from the earliest period of settlement. It is likely that they took advantage of the cross-Caribbean current and the calm waters of the Caribbean Sea to reach the islands.

Other prerequisites to successfully colonize islands include horticulture, a marine economy, a material culture that uses shell as a major raw material resource, and the ability to change an island's resource base by introducing plants, animals, and assets through exchange. Since 500 BC, all West Indian cultures have met each of these requirements.

TAÍNO WORD	TRANSLATION
Maca	Large tree for making canoe
Piragua	Carib canoe with sail
Cayuco	Flat boat with no keel (raft)
Caya	"Towards island," pass between islands
Nahe	Paddle

In the Caribbean islands, the direction of colonization generally followed the direction of the currents. The south equatorial current flows north from the Venezuelan coast up the Windward Islands. As it reaches the Leeward Islands it is eclipsed by the north equatorial current, which flows westward past the Leewards, paralleling the northern coasts of the Greater Antilles. The distances between the islands are not great, and once the 120-kilometer (75-mile) gap between Trinidad and Grenada was bridged, every other volcanic island was intervisible from the next with distances of less than 50 kilometers (31 miles). There was no fear of not finding the way home after setting out to investigate a new island.

Once you can navigate well, you possess the maritime skills to sail past one island to reach a better one. Thus, accessibility fails to be a determining factor. In the Pacific, where the distances between islands are much greater, colonization occurred in quite the opposite way; here, navigators sailed against the winds and currents when exploring in order to ensure that they could return home.

The ability to supplement the natural resources of an island with domesticated foods substantially reduces the risks involved in island settlements. When the Polynesians colonized a new island, they brought taro, sweet potato, fruit trees, and domesticated pigs and chickens. In the West Indies, in addition to root crops and some fruit trees, the colonizers brought with them dogs and small mammals such as guinea pigs for food. They also transported West Indian species, such as hutias (a large rodent) and rails (a ground bird, some species of which are flightless), from one island to another. Sweet potato may have been a key ingredient in island colonization by horticulturists, because it produces an edible crop in two months or less, quickly establishing a reliable food base. The Taíno were known to plant the root crop manioc on uninhabited islands, but never settle the island, creating food stocks for voyagers or for times of shortage.

The Turks & Caicos Islands were first colonized about AD 700 by peoples

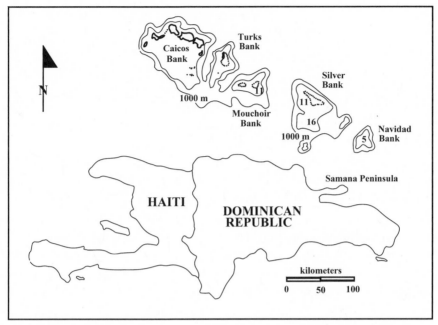

24. Map showing the shallow banks north of Hispaniola. Early voyagers following the banks would have been led straight to the Turks Bank and the island of Grand Turk.

coming from Hispaniola. So, how did the navigators of Hispaniola stumble upon Grand Turk first? As you head north from the coast of the Dominican Republic, you encounter within forty miles a series of shallow banks: Navidad, Silver, and Mouchoir. They are submerged under five to sixteen meters (sixteen to fifty-two feet) of water today.

These shallow banks may have given the appearance of islands on the horizon by virtue of their aquamarine color, and the banks themselves could have attracted fishermen to their abundant marine resources. If voyagers from Hispaniola explored this line of banks looking for dry land, they would have been led to the Turks Islands, and Grand Turk is the largest island on this bank.

The northwesterly Antillean current flows from Puerto Rico toward the Bahama archipelago, eventually joining the Gulf Stream. This, in association with the tradewinds, which blow east to west, would promote drift voyaging in the northwest direction, making voyaging from eastern Hispaniola to the Turks easy, but return voyaging more difficult.

The navigators of the Caribbean were not, however, at the mercy of the winds and currents of the region. The winds blow east to west in the summer and more northeast to southwest in the winter. All maritime cultures have a vast under-standing of winds and weather systems. The Spanish recorded just one Taíno word for wind, *huracan,* which described only the fiercest winds. The language of the modern Miskito Indians of coastal Nicaragua has twenty-five words to describe types of winds. For the Miskito, the dry season, when tradewinds are less intense and no unexpected squalls or storms occur, is the time of the long-distance journey. For the West Indies, February through April, with multiple day-long intervals of still weather, are the driest months and perhaps the best time for long distance trav-els. At the Governor's Beach site on Grand Turk, where people from Haiti came to make shell beads in the thirteenth century, all of the clamshells have growth lines that indicate they were harvested during this season. This suggests that the Taíno also recognized this as the best time period to travel over open waters.

Besides the ability to navigate well, the key technology for any complex island society is advanced water transport consisting of sophisticated ocean-going vessels that can carry large cargo loads and travel long distances. Large canoes allow for the distribution of wealth and the amassing of populations for military and cere-monial events.

The Taíno possessed canoes of various sizes and proportions for different ac-tivities. Small canoes may have been individually owned, but some larger, special-purpose canoes could have been shared by a community and had restricted access. Because of this, the most important factor in choosing a settlement was access to the open ocean. They needed launching and beaching places for their large canoes.

The dugout canoes constructed by the Taíno were made from the trunk of a single large tree (*maca*), although the sides may have been built up with planks to allow for construction of very large vessels. The Spanish chroniclers described im-mense Taíno *canoa.* Las Casas said the canoes in Cuba were twenty meters (sixty-five feet) long, and Columbus reported seeing very large canoes under sheds on the south coast of Cuba. Oviedo wrote that the boats had cotton sails, but this is gen-erally not believed to be a pre-Columbian trait.

The Island Caribs in the seventeenth century did have boats with sails (called *piragua*), but again this was likely due to European influence. Today, the tradition of handcrafted boats is best seen in Haiti where types of boats range from rafts to dugouts to sloops (see plates 14 and 15). The Taíno had a word for a flat boat with no keel (*cayuco*) that may have resembled a raft.

Las Casas noted that the Mona Passage between Hispaniola and Puerto Rico was the site of daily voyages, and thus culturally more closely linked than eastern and western Hispaniola. So, the primary movement of people and goods in the Greater Antilles was between water passages, and not within an island's landmass. The word for the passage between small islands was *caya*. The Taíno maintained gateway communities or outposts such as MC-6 on Middle Caicos, which allied far-reaching political territories and greatly increased trade opportunities. This is evidence that the Taíno were voyagers and were not isolated on their separate islands.

There is only one preserved Lucayan Taíno canoe. It is very small, about two meters (six feet) long, and was found in a blue hole on Andros Island in the Bahamas. In addition, two canoe paddles (*nahe*) have been recovered. The first was found in a cave on Mores Island, near Abaco, on the Little Bahama Bank. The second paddle was found in the peat sediments of North Creek on Grand Turk and is nearly identical to the first; it currently is on display at the Turks & Caicos National Museum. Las Casas described Taíno paddles "like long handled bakers' shovels, but sharp." The Mores paddle was first described in 1913 by Theodoor de Booy and remains the only other prehistoric paddle known from the Bahama archipelago.

The Grand Turk paddle was carved from a single piece of bullwood, a native to Cuba, Hispaniola, and the northern Bahamas. This species is not known from the Turks & Caicos Islands today. The paddle may have been carved in Hispaniola and lost after working its way to Grand Turk along with the first inhabitants of the island. The wood was radiocarbon-dated and provided a calibrated age range of AD 995 to 1125, centuries after Grand Turk was first colonized. This suggests that people sailed between Hispaniola and the Turks & Caicos Islands regularly and for many centuries.

The cultural history of the Lucayan Islands includes occupations by Taínos, Bermudians, Loyalists, and post-Emancipation period Africans who were formerly enslaved to work in the salt and cotton industries in these islands. What these cultures had in common was the island environment. All these people had to make a living from the sea, and their lives were intimately tied to boat technology. There is one indelible reminder of this in the history of the Lucayan Islands—boat images scratched into the plaster of ruinous plantation houses throughout the Bahamas and Turks & Caicos Islands.

Etchings of sailing vessels have been found throughout the Bahamas and have been reported on plantation ruins from New Providence, Crooked Island, and San Salvador as well as Middle and North Caicos and Providenciales. Laurie Wilkie and Paul Farnsworth (2005), who have worked on plantations throughout this re-

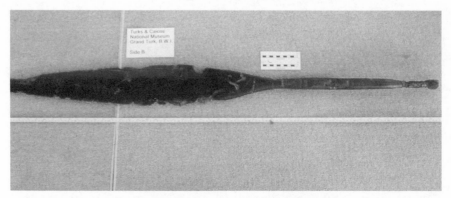

25. Canoe paddle from the Coralie site, Grand Turk. Photo by Brian Riggs (used by permission).

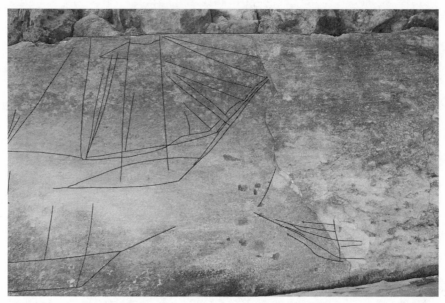

26. Photo of ship etchings in doorframe of Turks & Caicos Loyalist Plantation. Lines digitally enhanced. Photo by Lisabeth A. Carlson

gion, argue that ship imagery is an important symbol in many contexts throughout the African Diaspora and link the drawings to the late enslavement period or post-Emancipation (*circa* 1820 to 1900).

In many cases, when the Loyalist plantations were abandoned the former slaves were left in the islands. They took residence in their former slave houses and plantation houses. The ship imagery in the ruins lends itself to a feeling of isolation, which we can imagine reflects what the freed slaves may have felt in these surroundings. Eventually, people congregated in small villages rather than live in isolation on the former plantations, and they turned to the sea to form a maritime rather than a primarily agricultural economy.

The etchings contain an amazing amount of detail—so much so that the specific type of boats depicted can be deciphered. The most common wooden boats of the time were a small ketch, single mast sloops, and schooners. A schooner has two or more masts and fore and aft rigging, which means the sails run with the long axis of the boat. Bahamian schooners could be up to fifty feet long and carry twenty men. A two-masted schooner is shown in the etching from a Turks & Caicos plantation ruin, along with fragments of two other boats. The ship likely had topsails, as is indicated by several horizontal lines near the top of the masts. All three ships have sprits extending off the bow with indications of multiple jib sails. The complete etching appears to have three jibs. Also illustrated are the fore sail (in the center of the ship) and the main sail (at the stern end of the ship).

The people making these drawings had intimate knowledge of the workings of sailing vessels. The commonness with which these images are found throughout these islands and the detail they show reinforce the bond all inhabitants of the Bahama archipelago had with the sea. It is this tie to the ocean environment that links all the prior residents of these islands as one.

16
Partying, Taíno Style

Music and dance are integral parts of human life. Every culture in the world has songs and dances that are used to mark important occasions and special ceremonies. Among the Taínos these were called *arieto*.

Taíno communities are characterized by the arrangement of houses around a cleared central space. Dancing and singing associated with communal ceremonies were most often conducted in this central plaza. One of the most important ceremonies was the autumn feast. Men and women wore wreaths of grasses and flowers on their heads and strings of shells on their arms, hips, and legs; and in the Lucayan Islands they are said to have worn crowns made of feathers. The ceremony began with a procession into the central plaza with the people dressed in little more than their ornaments, although married women wore a short skirt made of woven cotton. During this ceremony food was offered to the *cemís* (*cemís* are both spirits and objects that represent spirits). The shamans (*behique*) would give a small piece of the cassava bread, which had been offered to the spirits, to each of the participants. These pieces were carefully preserved until the following year (much as Catholics keep palm leaves from Palm Sunday until the following Easter). Their singing and dancing was accompanied by drumbeats.

Drums were used only on the most solemn of occasions. These included celebrating the deeds of the ancestors, preparations for war, and ceremonies associated with marriage and death. Men and women danced by themselves in rows or circles with their arms around the waist of their neighbors. The songs that were sung were part of their sacred knowledge passed down from the chiefs to their successors.

TAÍNO WORD	TRANSLATION
Arieto/Ariete	Ceremonial song and dance
Cemí	Spirit of the dead and an object that represents a spirit
Behique	Shaman
Uicu	Cassava "beer"
Chicha	Corn "beer"
Cohoba	Narcotic snuff
Batey	Ball game
Gioia	Narcotic herb
Maguay	Wooden drum
Maraca	Gourd rattle

These songs—oral histories—sang the praises of the gods and the heroic deeds of the ancestors. Each song could last three to four hours, and the dancing continued until the dancers collapsed from exhaustion and intoxication, the latter the result of consuming copious quantities of "beer" made from either fermented cassava (*uicu*) or fermented corn (*chicha*).

During some ceremonies the chiefs would inhale a narcotic snuff made from the crushed seeds of the piptadenia tree. The snuff (*cohoba*) was placed on a platform atop a carved wooden statue representing the *cemí* with whom the chief wished to communicate. By entering a trance, the chief was able to ask the spirit for special assistance and to divine the future. These visions set the course for future actions. At times, this was accompanied by the playing of a ball game, called *batey*. The game consisted of two opposing teams of ten to thirty players who attempted to move a spongy "rubber" ball the length of the court without using their hands or feet. Both sexes played the game, but always separately. The outcome of the game could be used as a public justification for community-wide decisions on a proper course of action. One chronicle records a particular game in which the life of a captive Spaniard hung in the balance; life or death depended on the outcome of the game.

The importance of *arieto* as sacred knowledge is apparent in early Spanish attempts to establish control and extract tribute from the Taínos. Faced with insatiable demands from the Spanish, the Taínos organized a war party consisting of over six thousand men under the leadership of the cacique Guarionex with the in-

27. This Taíno table used for inhaling *cohoba* was carved in the form of a bird. Found in a cave in Jamaica. Photo by William F. Keegan.

tention of wiping out the Spanish colony at La Isabela. Bartholomew Columbus received advance warning of the planned attack and, in violation of Taíno rules of behavior, attacked after dark and captured the caciques that were directing the rebellion. The caciques, including Guarionex, were released after promising never to rise up against the Spanish again. However, shortly thereafter Columbus realized that he had made a mistake and sought to take Guarionex as his captive.

Guarionex had gone into hiding among the Macorix (a group on Hispaniola who spoke a language different from Taíno). The Spanish demanded that Mayobanex, the cacique of the Macorix, turn over Guarionex. Although his sub-chiefs argued that Guarionex must be surrendered to avoid war with the Spanish, Mayobanex could not bring himself to do so. He replied that it was not reasonable to give him up to his enemies since he was a good man, had wronged no one, had always been his friend, and had even taught Mayobanex and his wife how to do the "*Arieto* of Magua" (where Guarionex's province was located), a ceremony that was highly valued. This act of defiance was too little too late. By 1504 all of the principal chiefs, including Guarionex and Mayobanex, had been deposed by the Spanish. Nevertheless, it is telling that sharing the sacred knowledge contained in the *Arieto* of Magua was considered a principal justification for loyalty.

Singing was also an important part of curing ceremonies performed by the *behique*. Called to exorcise the evil spirit that had invaded the body of a desperately ill person, the *behique* would use a bone or wooden spatula (often carved at one end to represent a Taíno *cemí*), to induce vomiting and thus purge the body of profane contents. The *behique* then inhaled *cohoba* or swallowed a narcotic herb (*gioia*) that allowed them to communicate with the spirits. After lighting a torch they danced and sang around the body accompanied by the rhythmic shaking of a rattle. After some time an object was removed from the body and was identified as the cause of the illness. If the individual recovered, the reputation of the *behique* was enhanced and the object was kept as a *cemí*.

A variety of musical instruments were used during *arieto*. As mentioned, the most solemn occasions were accompanied by the beating of a wooden "tongue drum." These drums, called *maguay*, were made entirely of wood and lacked the animal-hide head that is typical of other drums (the Taínos had no large mammals from which to make drumheads). The drum was beaten with a single wooden stick, and provided the beat that was followed by the singers and dancers. For their part, the dancers wore strings of shells that "tinkled" together with the rhythm of their movements. Based on archaeological finds these seem to have been made mostly from Olive shells. It has also been suggested that women played a sort of castanet, which may have been made from opposing clamshells.

The Taínos also had rattles, as mentioned in conjunction with the curing ceremonies of the *behique*. Although the Spanish described these as made from wood, it is more likely that they were hollowed-out tree gourds. Two types of *maraca* are described. The first was small and held in both hands, which suggests that they lacked a handle. The second had two handles, described as scissor-like, and were much larger. We know that gourds were used as water containers so these may have been used primarily when calling upon spirits associated with water. In addition, some of the earliest pottery bowls in the Caribbean have hollow "adornos" affixed to the sides that contain small clay pellets that cause them to rattle when shaken. Adornos typically represent animals in at least two perspectives. The animal associations with particular spirits may have carried over to the more prosaic use of undecorated rattles. Alternatively, these rattles, which typically are not preserved in archaeological sites, may have had incised decorations representing particular *cemís*.

We know that trumpets made from the shells of large marine snails were used for signaling, and examples of shell trumpets are well known from archaeological excavations in the islands. Moreover, the making of a shell trumpet cannot be accomplished through the simple smashing of the uppermost point of the shell. The apex of these snails is far too hard and dense to create a useful mouthpiece, so the uppermost portion had to have been carefully removed. What is surprising is that we have found trumpets made from a variety of different large snail shells and in a variety of different sizes. Each of these would yield a different tone that could reflect differences in the signal being presented, but may also reflect the use of trumpets as a musical accompaniment to particular *arieto*.

One of the most spectacular trumpets that we have found was recovered from the Governor's Beach site on Grand Turk in the Turks & Caicos Islands. What is remarkable is that this small Atlantic triton shell had been used to the point where the ridged surface of the shell was worn flat where the person blowing the trumpet held it in their fingers. After cleaning the shell and experimenting with its use as a trumpet, we found that it would only emit a sound if held with fingers placed exactly on the worn surfaces. It is hard to imagine why such a long-used and apparently prized instrument was discarded, especially when it still worked perfectly eight hundred years later!

One of the most enigmatic musical instruments is the bone flute. Although few have been found in archaeological contexts, and the Spanish chroniclers provide only passing mention of their use, their existence cannot be denied. Interestingly, the Harn Museum of Art at the University of Florida has a collection of eight such flutes that were donated by a private collector. Dr. Peter Roe, a well-regarded authority on Taíno mythology and iconography (1997), examined these and concluded that they were authentic. The bone flutes are made from human leg bones and have open ends with holes drilled along their central axis. The occasions on which such flutes were used is not described by the Spanish.

The brass bells that were brought by the Spanish fascinated the Taínos. This in part comes from the Taíno association of gold or brass objects with a heavenly source (*turey*). Columbus's most desired trade items were small hawks' bells (bells attached to the feet of hawks trained for hunting). In addition, the brass church bell at La Isabela was highly esteemed as "*turey* that speaks," because the peal of this bell called the faithful Christians to mass.

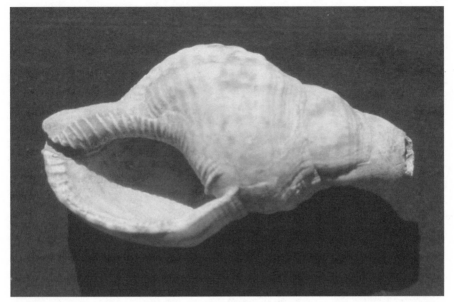

28. Trumpet made from the Atlantic triton shell. Excavated at the Governor's Beach site on Grand Turk. Photo by Corbett McP. Torrence (used by permission).

The term *arieto* tends to be associated with formal occasions, yet Las Casas noted that women would spontaneously break into song as they worked together on the drudging task of processing manioc into cassava bread. Thus, while scientists may try to attribute logical and/or sacred meanings to such frivolous activities as singing and dancing, we cannot deny, "music hath charms to soothe the savage breast."

17
Caves

THE ISLAND [Hispaniola] has a section called Caonao in which there
is a mountain called Cauta and it has two caves, Cacibajagua, CAVE OF
THE JAGUA, and Amayaúna, CAVE WITHOUT IMPORTANCE. From
Cacibajagua came most of the people who inhabit the island.

—Ramón Pané, 1496; translated by
Antonio Stevens-Arroyo (1988)

The first physical evidence for the native peoples who inhabited the Bahama archipelago was discovered in caves. When Julian Granberry wrote the first summary of Lucayan archaeology in 1956, he noted that 45 of the known sites were in caves and only 16 were in open-air settings. All but one of those 16 open-air sites was in the Caicos Islands. Today, there are about 111 cave sites and almost 400 open-air sites recorded for the Bahama archipelago.

The early discovery of cave sites resulted not only from the Taínos fascination with caves, but also from the extensive excavations of cave earth (bat guano) for use as fertilizer in the nineteenth century. During these excavations, pottery, exotic stone *cemís,* human burials, wooden objects (including fishhooks, bowls, and carved chiefs' chairs or stools called *duhos*) were recovered and petroglyphs (engraved images) and pictographs (painted images) have been observed throughout the Caribbean. The Taíno word for cave was *xaweye.* Although they may have used them as shelter from severe storms, the Taínos did not live in caves. The materials observed and recovered from caves indicate a far more spiritual association; one that is reflected in part in the epigraph concerning their mythology.

Caves are common in the karst (limestone) landforms found throughout the Caribbean. They occur in two forms. Sea caves have formed where wave action has undercut rocky cliffs and bluffs along the shore. Due to their proximity to the sea the Taínos used very few of these caves. Of greater importance were caves in the interior ridges of the islands formed through the dissolution of the bedrock, usually beginning along fault lines in the rock where acidic rainwater easily dissolves the

TAÍNO WORD	TRANSLATION
Duho	Chief's chair/stool
Xaweye	Cave
Xara	Lake
Xawei	Sinkhole
Potiza	Ceramic water bottle
Haba	Basket
Makuto	Deep basket
Macana	War club

limestone. These caves typically have two components: vertical sections created by the downward flow of rainwater, and horizontal sections created by the flow of underground streams. The highest rate of dissolution occurs on the margins where underlying salt water mixes with the overlying freshwater lens, creating what geologists call "flank margin caves." In these caves, rounded tunnels are spaces that once were completely filled with water, while triangular and rectangular tunnels result from streams running across the floor.

Caverns are large openings where several tunnels meet. They often have very high ceilings with substantial amounts of collapsed rock from the roof lying on the floor and multiple openings in the ceiling. Lakes (*xara*) can occur where the depth of the cave reaches the water table. The longest explored underwater cave system in The Bahamas is Lucayan Cavern on Grand Bahama Island with passages extending for more than five miles. In the Turks & Caicos Islands, the most spectacular cavern is Conch Bar Cave on Middle Caicos.

There is nothing quite like being deep in a cave and turning off your flashlight to be surrounded by complete and utter darkness, duck-walking through a low and narrow chamber as thousands of bats rush past you to escape your approaching light, or entering an interior chamber with the floor alive with scurrying cockroaches and cave crickets.

The Taínos used caves as sanctuaries for ritual purposes. Taíno cosmology recognizes three main divisions: a sky world, the land world of living people, and the world of subterranean waters. Caves were the portals to the subterranean world. As the myth at the beginning of this chapter tells us, the Taínos believed that all humans shared a common origin. However, only the origin of the Taínos was considered important. They had emerged from *Cacibajagua* (Cave of the Jagua), a reference to the *jagua* tree, whose edible fruit produces a black vegetable dye used for body painting. In contrast, the Cave of *Amayaúna* is translated as the "cave without

29. Painted Taíno image (pictograph) in cave in Parque Nacional del Este, Dominican Republic. Photo by William F.
Keegan.

importance." Apparently, the Taínos are the one true people who emerged from the
sacred cave, while the rest of humanity came from some place of no importance!

The importance of caves in Taíno mythology is expressed in their association
of animals that frequent or live in caves with spirits of the ancestors. Bats and owls
are especially important in this regard because they live in caves and are active at
night when the world of the living is replaced by the world of the dead. Moreover,
the decoration of cave walls with petroglyphs and pictographs enhanced the ritual
significance of these passages to the underworld. Petroglyphs have been reported
from only one cave in the Turks & Caicos Islands. This cave is located near Jacksonville Harbour on East Caicos and was visited by Theodoor de Booy in 1912 when
the East Caicos Sisal Company was in operation and bat guano was being excavated from a number of caves. Several efforts to relocate the petroglyphs have been
unsuccessful. There are no cave paintings reported for the Bahama archipelago.

30. Petroglyphs recorded in 1912 by Theodoor de Booy near Jacksonville, East Caicos. Reproduced from *American Anthropologist* (1912), N.S. 14, p. 103.

The symbolism in these carved and painted images is difficult to interpret, but they include both anthropomorphic (human forms) and animal imagery. Hartford Cave on Rum Cay in The Bahamas is one of the most elaborately decorated and included a petroglyph representation of a canoe paddle (until it was hacked out of the wall and brought to the New World Museum on San Salvador!). Painted images on the walls of caves in the Dominican Republic are especially evocative. One scene depicts the *cohoba* ritual in which the cacique ingested a hallucinogenic snuff to induce a trance that facilitated his communication with the spirits. When viewed in the flickering of torchlight the images appear to come alive.

One of the questions we frequently are asked is, "Where did they bury their dead?" Unfortunately, we do not have a complete answer. In some places the Taínos buried their dead in cemeteries. The dead were buried beneath the central plaza at the sites of Maisabel in Puerto Rico and El Chorro de Maíta in Cuba (Valcárcel and Rodríguez 2004). Knowledge of previous burials at Maisabel was so complete that despite hundreds of interments over a period of eight hundred years not one disturbed a previous burial (Siegel 1992). Evidence for formal cemeteries is lacking

31. Petroglyphs recorded in 1912 by Theodoor de Booy on Rum Cay, Bahamas. Reproduced from *American Anthropologist* (1913), N.S. 15, p. 4.

from the Bahama archipelago. To date, all of the burials in the Bahamas have been found in caves.

Blue holes and sinkholes, caves whose vault has collapsed to expose subterranean lakes, are also associated with ritual activities. The Taíno word for sinkhole (*xawei*) is very similar to their word for cave (*xaweye*). Cottage Pond on North Caicos is a perfectly circular inland blue hole that measures 165 feet across and sits in a beautiful natural depression that supports rare plant and animal species. It has a thirty-foot layer of freshwater that was certainly valued by the Lucayan inhabitants.

In the Bahama archipelago human burials have been found underwater in caverns and blue holes on Grand Bahama, Abaco, Andros, Eleuthera, and Providenciales. In addition, the extremely well-preserved skeletons of crocodiles, tortoises, and birds were recently found in a sinkhole on Abaco. The most spectacular finds have come from Parque Nacional del Este in eastern Dominican Republic where Geoff Conrad, John Foster, and Charles Beeker (2000) have investigated a number of underwater caves and caverns. This region of Hispaniola is quite arid, and water sources are limited. It is therefore not surprising that a substantial number of ceramic bottles used to collect water (*potiza*) have been found in flooded caverns. Yet water collection was not the only activity associated with these flooded caverns and sinkholes. Divers have also found decorated pottery bowls that are poorly suited for water collection. And the objects recovered from the Manantial de la Aleta flooded cavern are reminiscent of the sacred cenote at Chichen Itza (the Mayan city on the Yucatan Peninsula). A wide variety of objects were "sacrificed" in the Aleta sinkhole, and the anoxic (lacking oxygen) waters surrounding the finds have resulted in a remarkable state of preservation. Along with pottery vessels, stone tools, complete baskets, cordage, wooden handles for stone axes, and a war club have been observed in the sediments at the bottom of this sinkhole. There are at least two Taíno words for different types of baskets, *haba* and *makuto,* and wooden war clubs were called *macana.* To date, only a few of the objects have been retrieved from this sinkhole because they require special conservation techniques that are of limited availability in the Dominican Republic. This discovery has opened an entirely new vista into the world of the Taínos.

Objects recovered from caves figured prominently in the early days of Caribbean archaeology. Over the years most archaeologists have turned away from caves to open-air sites where a more complete record of Taíno lifeways is preserved. With the development of new techniques for safely exploring submerged caverns and the development of formal techniques for studying rock art, these portals to the subterranean waters are once again receiving the attention they so richly deserve.

18
Birds of a Feather

[The men] were very anxious to have women, and on many occasions while it rained, they had sought to find traces of their women, but they were not able to find any news [of them]. But that day when they washed, they saw fall from some trees . . . a certain kind of persons, who were neither men nor women, nor had the sexual parts of either male or female. After they had captured the creatures, they took counsel about how they could make them women . . . They sought a bird whose name is Inriri . . . This bird bores holes in trees, [and in our language is called a woodpecker]. They took the women without sexual parts . . . and they tied their hands and feet. Then they took this bird and tied it to the bodies. Thinking that the creatures were logs, the bird began to do the work to which it was accustomed, boring open and pecking away at the place where the female's private is usually found. In this way, the Indians had women.
—Ramón Pané, 1496; translated by
Antonio Stevens-Arroyo (1988)

The Spanish recorded about forty Taíno names for birds. It is likely that there were many more named species, but that these did not catch the attention of the chroniclers. Some names were recorded because the birds were similar to those in Europe, so it has been possible to use the published descriptions to decipher their modern common and scientific names. Other birds were described and their names recorded because they were novel. For example, the insectivorous smooth-billed ani, a long-tailed, glossy black cuckoo with an extraordinary bill that is deep at the base with a high and thin ridge on top ("culmen"), still bears its Taíno name (*ani*).

Finally, some birds entered the lexicon through their prominent roles in Taíno mythology. The best example is the industrious woodpecker (*inriri*). By fashioning women from creatures without genitalia, this bird achieved everlasting esteem in the hearts and minds of men. Indeed, birds with long pointed beaks are relatively common in Taíno symbolic arts.

Oviedo claimed that there were "so many different species of parrots" that it would be tedious to describe them all. The Spanish recorded two Taíno words for parrot: *higuaca* for the larger amazon parrot and *jajabi* for a smaller parrot, per-

TAÍNO WORD	TRANSLATION
Ani	Smooth-billed ani
Inriri	Woodpecker
Higuaca	Amazon parrot
Jajabi	Small parrot (parakeet)
Guacamayo	Macaw
Guani	Bee hummingbird
Guacarigua or *zum-zum*	Hummingbird
Curua	Cormorant
Maubeca	Heron
Yaguasa	Great blue heron
Tujuy	Coot
Sora	Sora
Querequete	Nighthawk
Yaboa	Night heron

haps referring to parakeets. The beautiful feathers of parrots were an important part of Taíno vestments. The Taínos made feathered capes and crowns and used brightly colored feathers for other decorative purposes. A common type of stone pendant has both horizontally and vertically drilled holes. The string for suspending the pendant passed through the horizontal hole, and feathers were inserted into the vertical holes at the top and bottom of the pendant. These objects and feathers were traded widely through the Taíno realm. Although there are no native flocks of macaws left in the West Indies, they used to brighten the Taíno skies and their feathers were the most valuable of all. Macaws were called *guacamayo* by the Taíno.

While excavating sites on Middle Caicos in 2000 we lived in the two rooms of the Vera Hamilton Elementary School in Bambarra. True to his morning routine Keegan fixed a cup of coffee and sat on the front porch to watch the sunrise. It might have been just like every other morning if not for the visitors of the previous day. A representative of the Darwin Initiative (United Kingdom) and the director of the National Trust had visited them to consider adding the trail to MC-6 and the south coast to the Crossing Path trail and to look into the possibility of converting the schoolhouse into an interpretation center for tourists (the interpretation center was officially opened in 2006). They were very excited when they arrived because on the previous day they had seen a bee hummingbird on North Caicos. The male of this species is the smallest bird in the world. These birds had not been reported in the islands for many years, although Dr. Steadman found a related species in the fossil deposits at Indian Cave, Middle Caicos. So this morning the tiny black bumblebee that flitted between the small purple flowers of the clearing in front of the schoolhouse merited special attention. Its flight pattern was not that of a bee; it clearly was a bird. A bird like that described by Oviedo almost five hundred years earlier as "no larger than the end of the thumb. There is no person who sees it fly but that thinks it is a bumblebee. So swift in flight that it is as impossible to see its wings." The Spanish recorded the Taíno word *guani* for bee hummingbird.

The larger, aquamarine hummingbird was referred to by the Spanish as "ca-bellos del sol" and "rayos del sol" (literally, hair and rays of the sun). The crescent shape of the hummingbird's body along with its iridescent coloring gave it an association for the Taínos with a rainbow. Rainbows, more specifically the double rainbow, figure prominently in Taíno cosmology. The double rainbow was a bridge between the land, the sky, and the underworld, the three realms of Taíno cosmology. Caciques used the rainbow as a symbol of chiefly authority. In the Taíno name for the hummingbird (*guacariga*), we again see the designation *gua*. *Zum-zum* is another name for hummingbird.

Animals that move freely between the three realms of sky, land, and the underworld of subterranean waters were highly esteemed. Bats held a special significance because they emerge from caves, the portal to the subterranean world, and enter the sky at night; sea turtles emerge from the sea to nest on land; and birds, especially those that enter the water, hold a special place in Taíno beliefs. Fully one-quarter of the birds recorded by the Spanish are associated with water. These include the cormorant (*curua*), herons (*maubeca* and *yaguasa*), the coot (*tujuy*), and the sora (*sora*). Representations of water birds have been associated with the Taíno water goddess *Coatrisquie.*

In Taíno mythology there is a division between the Order of Fruitfulness and the Order of Inversion. Each must be served to ensure the delicate balance of nature. The chief female spirit or *cemí* of the destructive side of nature was *Guaban-cex.* She was the driver of wind and water and rider of the hurricane. She was accompanied by two other *cemís*—a herald and a sweeper. The former was thunder, named *guataúba,* the "b" in whose name should be pronounced as loud as possible to simulate the sound of a thunderclap. The latter was *Coatrisquie,* who gathered the waters and let them flow so they destroy the countryside. Birds that carry the bitter and destructive waters from the sea to the earth while passing through the sky represented her.

Night was a dangerous time. It was a time when only the *opía* or forest spirits

32. Owl images can be recognized on modeled pottery adornos. Example from Jamaica. Photo by Lisabeth A. Carlson.

were out and about. Again, night birds have a prominent place in the lexicon. These include nighthawks (*querequete*) and night herons (*yaboa*), along with owls (*mucaro*), which are of special significance because, like bats, they too frequent caves and caverns; their images appear on pottery vessels. And anyone who has spooked a yellow-crowned night heron will attest to the heart-stopping squawk emitted by this bird on a dark night. Imagine trying to sleep in a thatched hut with a yellow-crowned night heron walking across the roof!

Working outdoors has provided ample time to observe the birdlife in the West Indies. When we surprised stiltbirds on a dry lakebed, they commenced their broken-wing dance to lead us away from their nest. Cuban crows with their "parrot-like squawks and guttural jabbering" laughed at us as we conducted walkover surveys (Bond 1961, 164). We watched two baby hummingbirds in their tiny nest along the road to a site on Middle Caicos for the month it took them to mature and fly away. There was an osprey who every day at noon would land on the light pole near the Coralie site on Grand Turk and casually eat the fish he had just caught in North Creek while watching us excavate.

With very little effort it is easy to find excellent bird-watching spots in the West Indies. It also helps to have a good guidebook. The classic for the islands is *Birds of the West Indies* by James Bond (1961), the ornithologist who provided the name for Ian Fleming's 007 character. After World War II, Fleming retired from British Intelligence and built his estate, named Goldeneye, on the north shore of Jamaica. Fleming kept a copy of *Birds of the West Indies* on his kitchen table at Goldeneye, and in 1952 he used this name that was so familiar to him. The real James Bond didn't meet Ian Fleming until the early 1960s. If you happen upon a copy of the book with its original dust jacket take a look at the author's photo. The real James Bond bears a striking resemblance to a young Sean Connery. And if you can't remember the title of the book, just remember Bond, James Bond.

19
Cannibals!

And they say that this cacique affirmed that he has spoken with *Giocauaghama* [the chief God] who had told him that whoever remained alive after his death should enjoy the rule over them only a short time, because they would see in their country a people clothed which was to rule them and to slay them and that they would die of hunger. At first they thought these would be the Canibales; but reflecting that they only plundered and fled they believed that it must be another people that the *cemí* spoke of. Wherefore they now believe that it was the Admiral [Columbus] and the people he brought with them.

—Ramón Pané, 1496

Pané's account illustrates just how quickly Taíno attitudes changed. In the *diario* of his first voyage, Columbus reported that the Taínos thought that he was a *Canibale*. The fact that he took people aboard his ships and they never returned, that he was clothed and had exotic vessels and weapons, convinced them that he had arrived from some supernatural realm. The Taínos soon realized their mistake when Columbus established a permanent colony. Supernatural beings may arrive from time to time, but they do not settle permanently in the land of the living. The Spaniards were something much worse than cannibals.

Caribbean cannibalism is a complicated issue. On the one hand, we need to consider the actual beliefs and practices of the Taínos. On the other, we need to deal with the prevailing attitudes in Europe at the time. Let's start with the Europeans.

As the anthropologist Neil Whitehead noted, the focus on cannibalism reflects the "European pre-occupation with this subject, still evident today, rather than its overall sociological significance for Carib peoples." Indeed, there were a number of extracts from human flesh and bone that were used as "medicines" in sixteenth-century Europe. It is reported that spectators would arrive at public executions carrying cups with which to collect and drink the still warm blood of the person who was executed. These forms of cannibalism were more alive in Europe than they were in the native Caribbean. Anyone really interested in the European fascination with cannibals should read the essays of Michel Eyquem de Montaigne that were first published in 1580 (1967).

NAME	CULTURE	TRANSLATION
Caribe/Canibale	Taíno	"Fierce, brave, strong person"
Canima/Caniba	Spanish	People of the Great Khan
Kalina/Karina	Carib	"Manioc eaters"
Carib/Caribe	Spanish	Fierce, cannibal
Caribbean		Land of the Cannibals

The issue of cannibalism can be pushed back even farther. In the fifth century BC, the Greek philosopher/historian Herodotus invented a dialogue between a person from the city and one from the country. In this urban/rural conversation, the city dweller is appalled that the rural folk cremate the dead and then consume the ashes of the deceased. In response, the representative of the rural folk is equally appalled that people in the city bury their dead where their bodies are subject to any number of degradations by the creatures that inhabit the soil. The rural perspective is that consuming the remains of their fathers is a far more respectable treatment of the dead than burying them in the ground.

More recently, James Michener (1988) used the notion of "peaceful Arawaks" (Taínos) and "warlike (cannibal) Caribs" as a literary device to portray the battle between good and evil in the West Indies. In addition, some historians have suggested that the reason the Bahama archipelago was first settled was because these people were fleeing the Carib "cannibals" who supposedly were attacking the islands of the Greater Antilles. According to legend, the Caribs ate the Taíno men and married the widowed Taíno women.

The Island Caribs survived centuries longer than the Taíno and most of what we know about them comes from later European descriptions, especially those of Raymond Breton (1647). The Island Caribs of the mid-seventeenth century called themselves *Kalina* or *Karina,* which is translated as "manioc eaters." Surprisingly, the Island Caribs are for the most part archaeologically invisible. Based on the available evidence, two proposals have been put forward. The first suggests that Carib peoples from South America began colonizing the southern Lesser Antilles just prior to Columbus's first voyage (around AD 1450). The second proposes that the peoples who already were living in these islands adopted trappings of Kalina culture (from the Guianas) as a reflection of their strong association with these people. We lack the evidence to decide which is correct. If the Caribs did arrive in the fifteenth century, they cannot be blamed for forcing people to settle the Bahama archipelago, an event that happened seven centuries earlier.

The fierce reputation of the Island Caribs comes partially from the fact that they resisted the European invasion. In this regard they exhibited remarkable political acumen. When a French colony was established on their island they would go to the British and suggest an alliance for the purpose of removing these French colonists from their island. When the French were removed, and a British colony established, they would go to the French to help them eliminate the British. This strategy was successful until the British and French reached accommodation in the Treaty of Versailles. The last of the Island Caribs were then rounded up and shipped to Central America.

So where does the notion of cannibalism in the Caribbean come from, and why were the Spanish so anxious to apply it? There are no firsthand accounts or other evidence that the Caribs ever consumed human flesh (anthropaphagy). Yet Oviedo described the Caribs as follows: "The bow-using Caribs . . . eat human flesh. They eat all the men that they kill and use the women they capture and the children that they bear, if any Carib should couple with them, are also eaten. The boys that they take . . . are castrated, fattened and eaten." Despite this sort of propaganda and the modern popular culture images of bodies being boiled in large cooking pots, the notion of eating your enemy has always been more an emblem of ferocity than an actual practice, and this is true universally. It was a common practice to use human bone to make objects of power, and these could have been made from the bones of slain enemies or the revered bones of ancestors.

The Spanish came to associate all fierce people with the name Carib, which reflects the translation of the Taíno word. The term "Carib" appears on European produced maps of other territories including the Philippines.

Columbus first heard the rumor of "Caribes" and "Canibales" while sailing along the north coast of Cuba during his first voyage. While exploring the Baie de l'Acul on the north coast of Haiti, Columbus recorded that the highest mountain in this region was called Mount Caribata. It is likely that he never would have focused on these names if he had not been looking for the Grand Khan of Cathay (China) and asking the people he met for the whereabouts of the "Canima" or "Caniba" (which to him meant the people of the Grand Khan). At what point Columbus realized that he had reached a "New World," and not the islands off the coast of Asia, remains an open question. It is easy to see how Canima or Caniba was easily confused with Caribe and Canibale, especially when neither party spoke a mutually intelligible language.

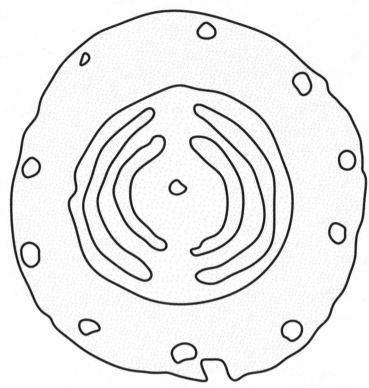

33. Line drawing of a perforated and incised belt ornament made from a human skull. Object in collection of the Museum del Hombre Dominicano, Bernado Vega Collection, Santo Domingo, Dominican Republic.

Columbus believed that the Caribe were the enemies of the Taínos, and he promised to defend them against this enemy. Yet the fact that Columbus first heard of these people in Cuba, and the people who came to be known as Caribs lived far to the south, suggests that for the Taínos the name was not associated with living peoples. The fact that the Taínos identified Columbus as a Canibale brings this distinction into sharper relief. If Columbus were a Canibale, then the Taínos must have lacked a corporeal knowledge of such beings.

On several occasions in his diario Columbus described the physical attributes of the Caribe/Canibale. They were described to him as "one-eyed men, and others, with the snouts of dogs, who ate men." What Columbus described are gods in the Taíno pantheon who are associated with the world of the dead. The dog god (*Opiyelguobirán*) guarded the world of the dead and carried their spirits into the afterlife. The Taíno notion of "eating men" can be interpreted as reflecting what happens after someone dies. Although their body remains intact, their spirit was consumed and carried over into the afterlife. In this regard it was not the actual consumption of human flesh, but rather the spiritual eating of the life force.

When Columbus encountered hostile natives in the Bay of Arrows (on the Samaná Peninsula of the Dominican Republic) on his first voyage, and on his second voyage on Guadeloupe and St. Croix, he concluded that these people must be Canibales/Caribes. In his mind, because they attacked him, they had to be the enemies the Taínos spoke about. Yet history is fraught with twists and turns. The peoples of the eastern Dominican Republic and St. Croix did attack the Spanish, but they were not Caribs, although the people he encountered in Guadeloupe may have been.

Columbus repeatedly told the king and queen of Spain that there were vast riches to be obtained from his enterprise of the Indies. Yet he continually asked for additional support from the Crown. When the promised riches failed to materialize, Columbus decided that enslaving the native peoples and sending them to Spain was a way to finance his colony. To their credit, the Spanish sovereigns returned the survivors of the first shipment of slaves back to Hispaniola, and they instructed Columbus to treat the native peoples as their vassals. In other words, they were to be given proper treatment, paid proper wages for their service, and converted to Christianity. These instructions were largely ignored, and the Taíno population of Hispaniola rapidly declined.

Faced with a significant shortage of native labor the Spanish colonists devised a new strategy. They told the Spanish monarchs that there were native peoples, known as Caribes or Canibales, who ate human flesh and refused conversion. In response, Queen Isabel proclaimed in 1503 that these "cannibals" could be enslaved. Suddenly, all of the native peoples of the islands were cannibals. This may explain why the Turks & Caicos and The Bahamas came to be known as the "Islands of Devils" and were the first to be entirely depopulated from slave raiding. Spanish predation, mistreatment, famine, and the introduction of diseases to which the local peoples had no immunities quickly led to the collapse of the Taíno peoples. Within twenty years of Columbus's first voyage, enslaved Africans were being imported to Hispaniola as laborers.

Were there cannibals (people who ate human flesh) in the Caribbean when Europeans arrived? Probably not. The Taíno notion of Canibales reflects their belief in what happened to the spirits of people after they died. The Island Caribs, and others, who resisted the Spanish invasion, were characterized as cannibals in order to justify their enslavement. There is no evidence that native West Indians consumed human flesh as a part of their normal diet, although the ritual consumption of cremated remains (endocannibalism) cannot be rejected. However, mixing the ashes of your parents in a drink is far less troubling to us than what was happening in Europe at the same time.

The notion of cannibals may be the product of Spanish misconceptions. However, during your visit to the Cannibal (oops, Caribbean) islands it is best to play it safe. Have a long talk with your waiter before you order the souse or steak-and-kidney pie!

20
Obeah and Zombies
The African Connection

Whenever we visit the Turks & Caicos Islands we try to get together with our old friend, Chuck Hesse, founder of the Caicos Conch Farm on Providenciales. And every time we see Chuck he promotes his belief that Africans were living in the Caribbean islands prior to the arrival of the Spanish.

The case for Atlantic crossings by Africans was first proposed on the basis of superficial resemblances between the physical appearance of black Africans and artifacts of the Olmec culture of Gulf-Coast Mexico. According to the Rutgers professor Ivan Van Sertima, the Olmec's colossal stone heads, terra-cotta sculptures, skeletal remains, and pyramids, along with ancient European maps, all point to contacts between Africans and Central Americans between 800 and 600 BC. Van Sertima's conclusions are not widely accepted, and little effort has been expended in searching for possible connections between the Taínos and Africa. Undeterred, Hesse is wont to point out that Taíno ceremonial seats are very similar to African birthing chairs.

The Taínos believed that their rulers were semi-divine and therefore should not contaminate themselves by sitting directly on the ground. Instead, they sat on low wooden seats called *duhos* that bear a striking resemblance to the low and sloping stools used in parts of West Africa during childbirth. Whether these resemblances are coincidental, derived from direct contact, or are the result of indirect contact remains to be demonstrated. The later possibility is at least partially supported by a wooden sculpture with Dahomey (West Africa) features that Keegan found washed up on a beach in Mayaguana (Bahamas).

While the jury is still out regarding possible pre-Columbian contacts between Africa and the Americas, there is increasing evidence that Taínos and other native peoples did interact with the enslaved Africans who were brought to the islands by Europeans beginning in the early sixteenth century. These interactions had a profound effect on cultural beliefs and behaviors that continue to the present.

We know that escaped Africans were adopted by Island Caribs in the Lesser Antilles and through miscegenation became the Black Caribs (Garifuna) whom the British rounded up, massacred, and then shipped the few remaining survivors to Belize at the end of the seventeenth century. A recent study conducted on Montserrat indicates that knowledge of some of the medicinal plants used by the Island Caribs was passed on to Africans and continues in use today.

The question of Taíno/African interactions is more difficult to specify because it has long been assumed that Taíno culture was extinguished by the mid-sixteenth century. More recent studies suggest that at least some Taínos managed to survive in remote areas. It is in this regard that two particular phenomena are worth reconsidering.

Let us start with a big tree. Columbus in 1492 and Oviedo in 1526 were both impressed by the size of the canoes that the circum-Caribbean Indians made from the ceiba (pronounced "sayba") tree. Ceiba (also called kapok or silk cotton) trees grow to more than one hundred feet tall and can measure ten feet in diameter above their buttress. The buttress can extend more than twenty-five feet from the base of the trunk. Taíno canoes were hollowed out of tree trunks all in one piece. Some were ten to twelve spans wide (a "span" measures nine inches or one-eighth of a fathom). The wood is exceedingly lightweight and easily worked. Dugout canoes are still made today from ceiba trees in Jamaica.

The Taínos also believed that the forest was inhabited by spirits of the dead and that one could identify these *opía* by the lack of a navel. They were reported to come out of the forest at night and feast on guava fruits. In fact, it is tropical bats that eat guavas at night, thus the Taíno association of *opía* with bats. *Opía* also are associated with the deities who ruled the world of the dead. According to Ramón Pané (1496): "They say a certain *cemí, Opiyelguobirán,* had four feet like a dog and is [made] of wood, and often he comes out of the house at night and enters the forests. They go there to seek him and bring him back to the house. They bind him with cords, but he returns to the forests."

Various beliefs in supernatural spirits were brought to the West Indies from Africa by enslaved peoples. It is likely that the last remaining native peoples also influenced modern beliefs. For example, one of the modern words for spirits of the dead—Obeah—may originally have come from the Taíno word *opía*. The anthro-

34. Wooden statue of *Opiyelguobirán,* the dog god who carried spirits to the world of the dead. Recovered from a cave in the Dominican Republic. In the collection of the Smithsonian Institution, Washington, D.C.

pologist Zora Neale Hurston studied Obeah in Jamaica for six months in 1936 and later published the book *Tell My Horse: Voodoo and Life in Haiti and Jamaica.* She reported that "duppies" (spirits of the dead) live mostly in ceiba and almond trees, and that neither tree should be planted too close to the house because the duppies will "throw heat" on the people as they come and go. Duppies are responsible for various kinds of mischief and can hurt a living person such that medicinal cures (including "balm baths") must be sought from local healers who serve as both "doctor and priest." Hurston's observations during a "nine night" ceremony (so named because it lasted nine nights after a person dies) are instructive:

It all stems from the firm belief in survival after death. Or rather that there is no death. Activities are merely changed from one condition to the other. One old man smoking jackass rope tobacco said to me in explanation: "One day you see a man walking the road, the next day you come to his yard and find him dead. Him don't walk, him don't talk again. He is still and silent and does none of the things that he used to do. But you look upon him and you see that he has all the parts that the living have. Why is it that he cannot do what the living do? It is because the thing that gave power to these parts is no longer there. That is the duppy, and that is the most powerful part of any man. Everybody has evil in them, and when a man is alive, the heart and the brain controls him and he will not abandon himself to many evil things. But when the duppy leaves the body, it no longer has anything to restrain it and it will do more terrible things than any man ever dreamed of. It is not good for a duppy to stay among living folk. The duppy is much too powerful and is apt to hurt people all the time. So we make nine night to force the duppy to stay in his grave." (Hurston 1990, 43–44)

Another connection can be found in the practice of vodoun (or voodoo), specifically with regard to the creation of zombies. The word zombi probably comes from the Kongo word nzambi, which glosses as "spirit of a dead person." In Haiti a zombi is someone who has annoyed his or her family and community to the degree that they can no longer stand to live with this person. They respond by hiring a bokor, a vodoun priest who practices black magic and sorcery. Through the application of a "coupe poudre" (magic powder) the victim appears to die. They are then buried and within a few days are exhumed. Though still living, they remain under the bokor's power until the bokor dies.

In 1982, the noted ethnobiologist Dr. E. Wade Davis (1997) went to Haiti following reports that two people who were supposed to be dead had recently returned to their villages. Both the victims and their relatives attested to the fact that these two had been turned into zombies. Fortunately for Dr. Davis one of the victims was able to describe the symptoms that followed his poisoning. Davis succeeded in learning the recipe for "poudre zombie" and was present to witness its preparation. In the process, he recognized that the main ingredients included "foufou," which we know as the porcupinefish, and the "crapaud de mer," sea toad or pufferfish. Both these fishes contain a deadly nerve toxin called tetrodotoxin.

But where did the use of pufferfish as a poison come from? It is not present in African versions of vodoun and must therefore have been added after Africans reached the Americas. The answer seems to be that Africans learned how to use this toxin from the Taínos. Indeed, there are substantial numbers of porcupinefish bones in the archaeological sites. Initially, we assumed that the Taínos had simply found ways to prepare the fish to avoid being poisoned. After all, their staple crop was bitter manioc, which is loaded with cyanide. If they had learned to remove one poison, they certainly could have learned to remove others.

We then made two discoveries that suggested these fish were not just food. First, the huge upper jaw of a porcupinefish was identified in a faunal sample from the site of MC-32 on Middle Caicos. This jaw was from a fish that would have been over two feet long, which is about their maximum size. The jaw was put on dis-

35. Close-up of porcupine fish. Photo by Barbara Shively (used by permission).

play in the original small exhibit of Taíno artifacts in the Turks & Caicos National Museum. By chance, it was juxtaposed to a display of pottery from local archaeological sites. One of the larger pieces was a portion of a bowl recovered from a site on Grand Turk, which was shaped like an animal. We originally thought that it represented a frog because frogs figure prominently in Taíno mythology. However, on closer inspection and comparison to published photographs of pufferfish, we became convinced that the bowl was shaped to look like a puffer. This bowl was brought to Grand Turk from Haiti around AD 1200. It was found in association with a variety of ritual paraphernalia in a place where the primary activity was the production of disk-shaped shell beads. These beads were woven into belts to record alliances between caciques, and their value derived from their brilliant red color and their origin across the sea.

The fish and the bowl both have a bulbous body, both have raised eyes, both have an elongated mouth, and both have nose holes—though the holes in the pot have been relocated to above the eyes where they served to accommodate strings by which the pot was suspended. Given the historical context in which this pufferfish effigy bowl was recovered, one is left wondering whether the Taínos used the tetrodotoxins in these fishes as a means to communicate with the spirits (as they did with *cohoba* and *tabaco*) and to heighten the authority of the shaman who could seemingly die and then days later appear to rise from the dead. Were there zombies before there was vodoun?

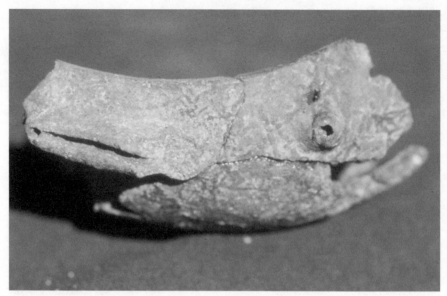

36. Pottery effigy vessel in the shape of a porcupine fish from the Governor's Beach site, Grand Turk. Photo by Corbett McP. Torrence (used by permission).

It has long been assumed that the Taíno peoples were driven to extinction prior to the arrival of enslaved peoples from Africa. However, new evidence suggests that there were interactions and that some of the Taínos's knowledge, beliefs, and practices have survived to the present. And maybe, just maybe, these interactions began centuries before the arrival of the Spanish.

21

The Stranger King

Este [Caonabó], fue valerosisimo y enforzado señor, y de mucha gravedad y autoridad, y segun entendimos a los principos a esta isla [Española] vinimos era de nacion Lucayo, natural de las islas de los Lucayos, que se pasó dellas acá, y por ser varon en las guerras y en la paz señalado, llegó a ser rey de aquella provincia [Maguana] y por todos muy estimado.

[Caonabó was a highly esteemed and powerful man, very serious and authoritative. We understand that he is one of the main chiefs of the island of Hispaniola. He is a Lucayan, who came from the Lucayan Islands. He is a man of war and peace, the King of Maguana, and is respected by all.]

—Bartolomé de las Casas

The tale of the "stranger king" is told in some version in virtually every culture in the world. It is the tale of an immigrant king who deposes a ruler, then solidifies the takeover by marrying the daughter of the former king. The basic story line is as follows: The heroic son-in-law from a foreign land demonstrates his divine gifts, wins the daughter, and inherits half or more of the kingdom. Before it was a fairy tale, it was a theory of society. Accounts of the stranger king have been retold numerous times in anthropological works. Marshall Sahlins (1985) devoted an extended essay to such beliefs, with an emphasis on those from Fiji and Hawaii and demonstrated how belief in a stranger king not only justified king/subject relations, but also structured native reactions during initial contacts with Europeans.

Caonabó was the most powerful cacique on Hispaniola when Columbus arrived on the island. It is likely that he grew up on Middle Caicos at the site known as MC-6. His story explores the intersection of myths, beliefs, and practices among the different participants who have written this history (see Keegan 2007). For example, the Taíno imbued Caonabó with a mythical status bordering on divinity; the Spanish imposed their own beliefs on their interactions with Caonabó and recorded the story; and the archaeologists who have studied this time period have used their beliefs to interpret the events and to present these as history.

The story and legend of Caonabó begins with the sinking of the *Santa María* off the north coast of Hispaniola. Shortly past midnight on Christmas Day, 1492, the *Santa María* had her belly ripped open on a coral reef. Awakened by the sound of an explosion that could be heard "a full league off" (about three miles), Columbus quickly assessed the situation and ordered the main mast cut away to lighten the vessel. He also sent Juan de la Cosa, the ship's master, to take a boat and cast an anchor astern in order to keep the vessel from being driven further onto the reef. Instead, de la Cosa fled to the *Niña*. The captain of the *Niña* refused to let de la Cosa onboard and sent a longboat to aid the admiral. It was too little too late; the *Santa María* was stuck fast.

The wreck of the *Santa María* occurred in the Taíno province of Marien, which was ruled by a cacique named Guacanagarí. Upon learning of the wreck Guacanagarí wept openly, and he sent weeping relations to console Columbus throughout the night. Afraid to risk the *Niña* in salvaging the *Santa María,* Columbus enlisted Guacanagarí's assistance. His people recovered everything, including planks and nails, and assembled the materials on the beach. So thorough were the Taínos that not a single "agujeta" (lace-end¹) was misplaced. Thus, Guacanagarí came to be the first Taíno cacique to establish a strong bond with the Spanish. Furthermore, his lifelong friendship with Columbus can be interpreted as an unsuccessful effort on his part to enhance his status in the island's political hierarchy.

Columbus took the sinking of the *Santa María* as a sign from God that he should build a fort in this location. Guacanagarí gave Columbus two large houses to use. With the assistance of his people, the Spaniards reportedly began the construction of a fort, tower, and moat in the cacique's village using the timbers and other materials salvaged from the *Santa María*. Because the *Niña* could not accommodate all of the sailors, about thirty-nine men were left at La Navidad with instructions to exchange and trade for gold.

When Columbus returned to La Navidad in 1493, he learned that all of the Christians were dead and that the fort had been burned to the ground. Columbus was told that soon after he returned to Spain the Spaniards fell to fighting among themselves. Some had gone off into the country to seek their fortune, but King Caonabó had murdered those who had remained there. History records that the Spaniards were killed because they abused the local people; they raped, looted, pillaged, and abused the hospitality of their hosts. Yet, if such local violations led to their deaths, then the local leader should have ordered the killings. Guacanagarí claimed that he was innocent, that he was a friend of Columbus, and that he had himself been wounded in battle defending the Spaniards.

Columbus apparently believed him, and he did not blame Guacanagarí for the destruction of La Navidad. Instead, Caonabó, the primary cacique for this region and the ruler to whom Guacanagarí owed fealty, was blamed. As proof, Columbus's son Ferdinand wrote that when Caonabó was later captured he admitted to killing twenty of the men at La Navidad. Would another leader have acted differently? Whatever abuses the Spanish may have committed, Caonabó could not allow a second-level cacique like Guacanagarí to harbor a well-armed garrison of Europeans in his village. Had he done so, his own survival would have been threatened.

The reaction of Caonabó to foreigners in his territory was immediate and swift. The fact that Caonabó took military action against the Spaniards at La Navidad attests to his status. Guacanagarí's village was more than eighty kilometers (fifty miles) as the crow flies (more than ninety kilometers [fifty-six miles] by foot) from Caonabó's village. Despite this distance, Caonabó exerted his power and displayed his regional status. Las Casas and Oviedo both identified him as one of the five principal caciques on the island. On his return to Hispaniola in 1493, Columbus was distracted by the need to establish a beachhead on the island, and thus Caonabó was ignored for a while. However, with the establishment of Fort Santo Tomás in the interior of the island, Caonabó and his brothers were again identified as the main threat to the Spanish enterprise.

In reading the accounts of the chroniclers it is hard to see why Caonabó was considered to be such a threat. Indeed, Carl Sauer (1966) concluded that Caonabó was not a menace. Furthermore, there reportedly was little gold in his cacicazgo, and there is no indication that he made any offensive moves against the Spanish after ridding himself of the pestilence at La Navidad. Perhaps his power and fame came from a reputation based on past deeds. It is possible that the Taínos who were being abused by the Spanish referred to their big and powerful brother (Caonabó) who would eventually come to their rescue. Or perhaps the perceived threat derived from Columbus's personal anger over the destruction of La Navidad. The motives are difficult to sort out.

Concerned with the threat that Caonabó posed to Fort Santo Tomás, Alonso de Hojeda and nine horsemen went to visit Caonabó as emissaries of Columbus. Hojeda was perhaps Columbus's strongest supporter, and the embodiment of the word conquistador. When Caonabó heard they were coming he was especially pleased because he was told they were bringing a gift of *turey*. When Hojeda arrived he told Caonabó that he had a gift of *turey* from Biscay (the location of the principal ironworks in Spain), that it came from heaven, had a great secret power, and that the kings of Castile wore it as a great jewel during their *arieto*. Hojeda then suggested that Caonabó go to the river to bathe and relax, as was their custom, and that he would then present his gift. Having no reason to fear a few Spaniards in his own village, Caonabó decided to claim the gift and went off to the river with a few retainers. While Caonabó was at the river, about two kilometers (one and one-fourth miles) from the village, Hojeda tricked him into going off with him. When the two were alone, Hojeda presented Caonabó with the highly polished silver-colored handcuffs and manacles he had brought. He instructed Caonabó in how they were worn and placed him on his horse; with Caonabó as his captive, Hojeda and his men (who had been nearby), with swords drawn, made haste to return to La Isabela. The trap was set and successfully sprung.

It is reported that Columbus decided to send Caonabó to Castile along with as many slaves as the ships would hold, although some dispute whether Caonabó was ever sent to Spain. The official report is that the ships sank and that Caonabó was lost at sea. It was further reported that Caonabó's brothers were determined to seek retribution by waging a cruel war against the Spaniards such that they would drive them from their lands. Yet there are no records of any substantial military successes by the Taínos of Hispaniola, so it appears that the brothers failed to achieve their reported objective. Within a decade, the native population was decimated by warfare, cruelty, enslavement, and disease.

Ferdinand Columbus described Caonabó as "a man well up in years, experienced, and of the most piercing wit and much knowledge." He was strong, authoritative, and brave. He was the paramount cacique for the Maguana *cacicazgo.* His main settlement was located on the west side of the Cordillera Central, and the Spanish town of San Juan de Maguana was established there after he was deposed. This town, which still exists today, is the site of the largest Taíno earthwork in all of the West Indies. It is today called "Corales de los Indios," and measures more than 125,000 square meters (thirty-one acres).

Caonabó was described as coming to Hispaniola from the Lucayan Islands. How was it that the most powerful chief in all of the Caribbean came from the relatively insignificant Lucayan Islands? That is a question for another book, but the fact illustrates how connected the people were throughout the far-flung Caribbean islands (see Keegan 2007).

Note

1. The closest modern example of an agujeta is the plastic tip at the end of a shoelace. At the time of Columbus's voyage, these were made of metal (often brass). At the site of El Chorro de Maíta in Cuba, dozens of brass agujeta have been found in association with human burials.

Anatomy of a Colony

A Taíno Outpost in the Turks & Caicos Islands

The Turks & Caicos Islands and Hispaniola were intimately connected during the Taíno past. This can be seen in settlements in the Turks & Caicos Islands that were occupied by people who lived most of the time in Hispaniola. Often these sites began as locations to extract economic items for use back home. They evolved into colonies as the Lucayan Islands became permanently settled.

One such site was located on the western shore of North Creek at the northwest end of Grand Turk. The Coralie site (GT-3) is one of the oldest archaeological sites in the Bahama archipelago and the first settlement in the Turks & Caicos Islands. It is also the best example of an initial colony on a previously uninhabited island in all of the West Indies. The site is located within twenty meters (66 feet) of North Creek, a large inland tidal creek or bay. About three hundred meters (985 feet) to the west is a sand beach above a shallow tidal flat (less than one meter [3.3 feet] deep), which extends for about five hundred meters (1,640 feet) to the barrier reef, beyond which the sea drops to two thousand meters (6,560 feet) in the Turks Island Passage. North Wells, a source of potable water for the past three hundred years, is about half a mile south of the site. It is likely that this low-lying area in which water collects today provided a relatively permanent water supply for the original inhabitants. The site is located where the residents could easily access prey in multiple habitats, such as North Creek, the ocean off the leeward side of the island, and on land. At this time in Grand Turk's history the terrestrial animals were large and plentiful.

The shore of North Creek is lined with red mangroves and sea purslane; the

37. Archaeological excavations at the Coralie site in 1996, Grand Turk. Photo by Lisabeth A. Carlson.

ocean shore is predominantly sea grapes; and dense acacia thorn brush and cacti, especially the prickly pear cactus, cover the dune itself. The current conditions, both botanically and zoologically, are a poor reflection of the past environment. Dr. Lee Newsom's study of wood charcoal from the site has revealed several trees that are today rare or absent from Grand Turk. These include wild lime, ironwood, Celastraceae (bittersweet family), and palm trunk wood. Buttonwood, which today grows along the margin of North Creek, was also present in charcoal samples. Moreover, clear growth rings of varying width and morphology are visible in charred wood samples, reflecting an annual rainfall regime of alternating wet and dry seasons.

The Coralie site was discovered in 1992 when prehistoric potsherds were exposed on the ground surface by land clearance for a housing development. To define its boundaries, a grid of shovel tests was laid over the site. These tests revealed a high incidence of sea turtle and other animal bones, pottery, and mollusk shells in low frequency distributed over a 40-by-150-meter (130 by 500 feet) area covering more than two acres. The archaeological deposits have been protected by burial under 30 to 60 centimeters (1–2 feet) of soil. Although we obtained one relatively early radiocarbon date (AD 900) from charcoal recovered in a test pit, it was only after we began to open larger areas of the site that we realized that this was a colony dating to the initial human colonization of the Lucayan Islands. Between 1995 and 1997, more than 250 square meters (2,700 square feet) were excavated in mostly contiguous units. Ten radiocarbon dates indicate that the site was occupied from about 1200 to 800 years ago (AD 705 to 1170).

The people who occupied this site were the direct ancestors of the Taínos. No skeletal remains have yet been found of the people themselves. What remains here is only what the people brought with them from Hispaniola, along with the bones of animals they butchered along this shoreline. Several pieces of polished greenstone, which had flaked off of celts or axes, and a nearly complete greenstone axe provide evidence that these were the first people to clear land on Grand Turk, probably for small gardens in which manioc, sweet potatoes, cotton, and other crops were grown. We also recovered a variety of conch, clam, and whelk shell tools, which could have been used in woodworking, preparing the land for cultivation, and processing turtles and fishes.

All of the more than eighteen hundred potsherds from the site contain mineral sand tempers. Because the Lucayan Islands are composed entirely of limestone, this pottery was imported from the Greater Antilles. Stylistically, the pottery is all of a style that archaeologists call "Ostionan Ostionoid." The style dates between AD 500 and 1200 in the Greater Antilles, and is characterized by fine red-slipped wares, coarse ware vessels, and griddles, all of which are common at the Coralie site. This site is the first of its kind with only Ostionan-style pottery north of Hispaniola.

This site contained fragments of classic Ostionan navicular (boat-shaped) bowls with strap handles arching above the rim. Turtle effigy bowls were identified from a red-painted appendage in the shape of a flipper and a wedge-shaped turtle face lug. The complete bowl would have had a turtle head lug at one end and four flippers arranged just below the rim of an oval vessel. This site functioned primarily as a place to capture and process turtle meat for local consumption as well as export, and it is interesting that the only animal images identified in the pottery were turtles. Finally, numerous thick griddle sherds were recovered. If complete, these griddles would have measured up to fifty centimeters (twenty inches) in diameter. The presence of griddles suggests that manioc was planted on this island and that cassava bread was being made on site. All the ceramics, including these griddles, had to have been transported to this island from Hispaniola, as no locally made ceramics were found in the site.

Most of the sherds show evidence of over-use, as if they were squeezing the last bit of life out of these imported vessels. The sherds from Coralie all lack dark cores, which indicates that they have been reheated many times. Such complete heating reduces the structural integrity of a vessel, causing it to break more easily. In the language of ceramic technologists, they become "friable." Several very large sherds in our excavations were so friable that they had the appearance and texture of popcorn. This situation shows that pots were in short supply.

The site is most notable for its unusual collection of animal bones, especially green sea turtles, which occur nowhere else in the region in such abundance. In addition to large quantities of turtle bones, we recovered the bones of very large rock iguanas, snakes, tortoises, many species of birds, and large fishes. Using the zoo-archaeological convention of estimating the minimum number of individuals, we counted at least 518 animals, 413 conchs, and 212 other mollusks in the one hundred kilograms (220 pounds) of bones and shells that were excavated. In terms of meat yields, 57 percent of the diet came from sea turtles, 24 percent from fishes, 12 percent from iguanas, 5 percent from queen conchs, and less than 1 percent each from birds, spiny lobster, and other mollusks.

The most common bird in the sample was the red-footed booby, a bush nesting species that often was extirpated when humans arrived in their territory. Today, there is only one nesting colony of red-footed boobies in all of the Lucayan Islands, but in the past they were common.

A surprising discovery was how many of the fishes were very large, including one 20-kilogram (40-pound) barracuda, and many 5-to-10-kilogram (10–20-pound) groupers, snappers, and rainbow parrotfish, along with some large sharks. These fish likely were captured using spears and/or hook-and-line technology. In that regard, Coralie differs from later sites where nets and traps are commonly used. The Coralie samples are also different in that large rainbow parrotfish (*guacamaia*) are the most common species of parrotfish in the site, while at all later sites in the Lucayan Islands the smaller stoplight parrotfish predominates. Also, the abundance of herring-size fishes found in other Lucayan Island sites are absent from the Coralie samples.

The faunal remains excavated at the Coralie site are substantially different from those at later sites, and reflect the richer diet available to those who are the first to settle a new area. As one would expect, the largest animals were consumed first, and the occupants of the site greatly benefited from being the first humans to exploit the pristine resource base. Even their food-processing techniques were adapted to the plethora of green turtles in their environment. A common feature in the site are hearths constructed from limestone rocks and conch shells on which a turtle carapace was used as the vessel in which turtle, iguana, and fish meats were cooked together. Surprisingly, very few mollusks were eaten.

38. Stone-and-conch-shell-lined hearth on which an overturned sea turtle carapace was used to cook a meal, Coralie site, Grand Turk. Photo by Lisabeth A. Carlson.

Compared to the heavily populated islands of the Greater Antilles, the uninhabited Lucayan Islands must have presented, economically, an incredible resource base for exploitation. It is because of the richness of these islands that the relationship between the Greater Antilles and the Lucayan Islands was maintained until the coming of Columbus.

23
Columbus, Hero or Heel?

Christopher Columbus—Admiral of the Ocean Sea, The Great Navigator—was renown as the champion of the belief that the earth was round. He sought the riches of the Far East by sailing to the west, and he happened instead upon a New World. The man who discovered America was removed from Hispaniola in chains in 1500 and wrongly persecuted in his later years. His story typifies that of a tragic heroic figure.

Yet how accurate is the portrait of Columbus that is painted today? How much of what we know comes from the deification of a long-dead hero whose personal attributes have been shaped to reflect the greatness of his discoveries? And how much of what we are being told today is simply a revisionist backlash that demands attention by attacking dead heroes?

A century ago Columbus was a hero who was feted in the Columbian World Exposition (Chicago 1893) as a man whose single-minded pursuit of his goals was to be emulated. Today he is often reviled as a symbol of European expansionism, the forebearer of institutionalized racism and genocide who bears ultimate responsibility for everything from the destruction of rain forests to the depletion of the ozone layer. These are impressive accomplishments for someone who died five centuries ago.

When one peels back the shroud of myth that today surrounds Christopher Columbus, we find that his portrait embodies a period of history more than it does an individual man. Robert Fuson (1987), a Columbus admirer, described him

39. Pigeon sitting on the head of the statue of Columbus in Parque Colón, Santo Domingo, Dominican Republic. Photo by Lisabeth A. Carlson.

as a man of the Renaissance, whose sensibilities were still firmly rooted in the Middle Ages.

An example of the Columbus mythology illustrates those points. Columbus is often credited with being the first to accept that the earth was round. Yet the Greek mathematician Pythagoras first proved this fact in the sixth century BC. Moreover, when Columbus obtained contradictory navigational readings off the coast of South America during his third voyage in 1498, he quickly abandoned his round earth. Instead, he proposed that the earth was shaped like a pear with a rise "like a woman's breast" on which rested the "Terrestrial Paradise" (Garden of Eden) to which no man could sail without the permission of God. To his detractors, such beliefs are those of a mentally unbalanced religious fanatic; to his promoters, they are remarkably prescient (the earth does in fact bulge along the equator) and they illustrate his steadfast and consuming faith in God.

Beyond historical attributes, his personal characteristics and life history add to the intrigue. What was his real name? Kirkpatrick Sale (1990) notes the following possibilities: Christoforo Colombo, Christofferus de Colombo, Christobal Colom, Christóbal Colón, and Xpoual de Colón. Columbus himself, after 1493, chose to sign himself Xpo ferens, which glosses as "the christbearer." As Saint Christopher had before him, he saw himself fulfilling God's plan by bringing Christ to a new world.

His place and date of birth are also uncertain. He was a Virgo or Libra (he was versed in astrology), born between August 25 and October 31, 1435 to 1460, with 1451 the most frequently given year. He claims to have been born in Genoa, although Chios (a Greek island that was a Genoese colony), Mallorca, Galicia, and other places in Spain have also been suggested. Wherever his place of birth, he seems to have thought of himself as a Castilian, the language in which he wrote.

His son Fernando described him as having a reddish complexion, blond hair (white after age thirty), blue eyes, an exceptionally keen sense of smell, excellent eyesight, and perfect hearing. Columbus was a man of relatively advanced age in 1492 (at least forty years old), and the description of him as having been in perfect physical condition must be an exaggeration. He was also reported to be moderate in drink, food, and dress, and it is said that he never swore! He was of the Catholic faith, although some claim a Jewish background on one side of his family. He expressed his faith in his choice of a Franciscan friar's robes for an appearance before the Spanish Court, in leaving his son at the Franciscan monastery of la Rábida between 1481 and 1491, and in his eschatological *Libro de las profecías,* an array of prophetic texts, commentaries by ancient and medieval authors, Spanish poetry, and Columbus's own commentaries (West and Kling 1991).

He is said to have gone to sea at age fourteen. On the Atlantic Coast to the north he made at least one voyage to England and possibly one to Iceland, while to the south he sailed as far as the Gold Coast of Africa. He is reputed to have been involved in a naval engagement between Franco-Portuguese and Genoese fleets in 1476. He made four voyages to the New World. Until recently, anything about Columbus's character, except his skills as a mariner, was open to criticism. Recently, revisionist historians are unwilling to grant even that. Kirkpatrick Sale claims that Columbus never commanded anything larger than a rowboat prior to the first transatlantic crossing. Yet it remains a fact that he succeeded in crossing the Atlantic Ocean and, more important, he returned safely. It was Columbus's voyage that set the stage for European expansion.

Columbus married Doña Felipa Perestrello e Moniz in 1479, and their son Diego was born in 1480 in the Madeira Islands. Doña Felipa died sometime between 1481 and 1485, after which Columbus consorted with Beatriz Enríquez de Arana. A second son, Fernando, was born to Beatriz in 1488. When Christopher served as governor of Hispaniola, he was assisted by his younger (or older) brother (or uncle) Bartholomew Columbus. Christopher, Bartholomew, and their other brother Diego were arrested in July 1500 for mismanagement of the colony. They were sent to Spain in chains in October and released in December of that year.

As one looks behind the historical facade that has been built to represent the "discoverer" or "destroyer" of America, one encounters many more questions than answers. The story seems to begin with Columbus seeking financial sponsorship for a voyage to Asia and the Indies. But was Asia really Columbus's objective? Henry Vignaud and others have maintained that Columbus pursued more personal goals. Upon reaching the islands Columbus spent two weeks searching for gold in the Bahamas. Why did he waste time in the Bahamas when his stated objective lay an apparent short distance to the southwest? Why did Columbus bring trinkets for trade if the gold of the Grand Khan was his primary objective? Why did Columbus claim lands for the Spanish Crown and himself as the Crown's representative, if these belonged to an Asiatic Kingdom? Why is there no mention of Asia or the Indies in the titles awarded to Columbus by his royal sponsors?

Christopher Columbus died on May 20, 1506, in Valladolid, Spain, of age-related causes. He was about fifty-four years old. Even in death Columbus left us wondering—Sevilla, Santo Domingo, and Havana all claim to be his final resting place. A fitting twist to the end of his story.

For five hundred years there has been only one answer to the question, who was Columbus? That answer is another question. Who do you want him to be?

24
One Small Step for a Man

To read Columbus's daily log (*diario de a bordo*) you would think that his small fleet was never very far from land. For thirty-two days after leaving Gomera in the Canary Islands on September 9, the diario makes repeated reference to signs of land. Sailing in the middle of the Atlantic Ocean, more than one thousand miles from the nearest land, Columbus observed "river weed" (sargassum seaweed), a live crab "not found more than 80 leagues [240 miles] from land," a booby or gannet, birds that "do not depart more than 20 leagues [sixty miles] from land," and "a large cloud mass, which is a sign of being near land." But it was not until two hours after midnight on October 12 that land finally did appear.

The land was an island, which the native Lucayans called Guanahaní. Scholars agree that Guanahaní is in the Bahama archipelago, but that is where agreement ends. To date, ten different islands have been identified as the first landfall; a truly remarkable number when you consider that only twenty islands in the entire archipelago are even remotely possible candidates. In addition, more than twenty-five routes have been proposed to take Columbus to the three other Lucayan Islands he visited before departing for Cuba. When represented on a single map, these routes look like someone gone mad playing connect the dots.

Cat Island, in 1625, was the first to be proposed as the landfall island. Cat went unopposed until Watling Island was suggested in 1793. Grand Turk was next, followed by Mayaguana, and Samana Cay in time for the four hundredth anniversary in 1892. Cat Island's claim was ably defended by the novelist Washington Irving, while Watling was promoted by the *Chicago Herald* (site of the Columbian Exposition in 1893), and Samana Cay was championed by Gustavus Fox, who served as assistant secretary of the navy under President Abraham Lincoln.

In 1926, Cat and Watling entered a legal battle over who had the right to use the name Columbus gave to the island where he first landed—San Salvador. The case was settled by the Bahamas legislature in favor of Watling. Known legally as San Salvador ever since, Watling gained its strongest support from the distinguished Harvard historian Samuel Eliot Morison, who retraced Columbus's steps in his 1942 Pulitzer Prize–winning biography of Columbus. Morison's reconstruction seemed to end the debate once and for all.

Other first landfall islands have been suggested since—Conception (1943), East Caicos (1947), Plana Cays (1974), Egg/Royal (1981), Great Harbour Cay (1990)—but none has made a sufficiently strong case to sway popular opinion away from Watling. None, that is, until 1986 when *National Geographic* magazine told forty million readers that Samana Cay was the place.

But why the debate? Why hasn't Guanahaní been identified with certainty? The answers lie in the quality of the evidence. The only detailed information concerning Columbus's first voyage is contained in his diario. Columbus presented the original to Queen Isabel, who had a copy made for Columbus. The whereabouts of the original is unknown, and all trace of the copy disappeared in 1545. What has survived is a copy made by Bartolomé de las Casas—a thirdhand manuscript handwritten in sixteenth-century Spanish that has numerous erasures, unusual spellings, brief illegible passages, and notes in the margins. The ambiguities, errors, and omissions in this manuscript have been compounded in modern-language translations.

Putting such problems aside for the moment, what of that account might be used to identify Guanahaní? Arne Molander, an advocate of Egg/Royal Island, has identified ninety-nine clues, many of which require specialized knowledge and most of which are subject to multiple interpretations. Such minutia is beyond the scope of this brief essay; instead let us consider four general categories: ocean crossing, descriptions of the islands, sailing directions and distances, and cultural evidence.

Using a computer-generated simulation of the first voyage that took into account prevailing winds and currents, the *National Geographic* team concluded that the crossing ended at Samana Cay (actually, they overshot Samana by more than three hundred miles and had to shorten their league by 10 percent to land at Samana). When a team from Woods Hole Oceanographic Institution substituted averages for prevailing winds and currents, their simulated crossing ended in sight of San Salvador (without need to adjust for distance). However, not satisfied with that solution, this same team plugged new numbers into their computer and put Columbus near Grand Turk! Too bad, as one reviewer noted, Columbus didn't have a computer on board.

A different approach to the crossing is to simply use Columbus's statement that Guanahaní was on the latitude of Ferro in the Canary Islands. Simple enough? Latitude sailing was certainly possible in Columbus's day, and Arne Molander has shown that the latitude from Ferro crosses Egg Island, just north of Eleuthera. However, Robert Power, armed with maps of the day, has shown that the Americas are consistently displaced northward on these maps and that in sixteenth-century cartography the line from Ferro crosses Grand Turk. In this way both northern and southern Bahamas landfalls have been supported.

The situation does not improve when you move to descriptions of the islands themselves. For example, prospective Guanahaní islands range in size from 10 to 389 square kilometers (4–150 square miles), the harbor that could hold "all the ships in Christendom" from 0.6 to 36.6 square kilometers (0.2–14 square miles), and the second island is either 5 by 10 leagues (as recorded in the diario) or 5 by 10 miles (a likely transcription error).

If we cannot be certain what he was describing, then we should at least be able to retrace how he got there. Yet the record of directions and distances has been used to defend more than twenty-five different routes. The most basic disagreements concern translation; such as whether "camino de" should be translated as "the way from" or "the way to." More complicated disagreements arise over interpolations. Between the night of October 17 and the morning of the nineteenth one route has the fleet sail fewer than twenty miles, while another has them cover more than three hundred. The first claims that bad weather prevented them from sailing on the eighteenth, while the latter claims that storm winds propelled the three ships at breakneck speed.

Lastly, Columbus visited four native villages and spent three days trying to reach the village of a chief. I have used archaeological evidence to show that the Watling to Rum Cay to Long Island to Crooked Island to Cuba route best fits all of the data. Others, however, believe that there were so many Lucayans living in the Bahamas that virtually every route will find archaeological sites in the places where Columbus observed villages. Only more archaeology will tell.

Where was Columbus's first landfall in the Americas? In our opinion, it is known today by the name Columbus gave it.

Although most expeditions expected to make port within two weeks, Columbus's three ships carried provisions for an entire year. Records of the 1498 voyage of the *Niña* listed stores of wheat, flour, wine, sea biscuit, olive oil, garbanzos, cheese, salt pork, vinegar, fatback, sardines, and raisins. Cooking was done on deck in large copper kettles over a fire in a sandbox kindled with vineshoots and fed with olivewood.

Because there is little mention of weapons in the earliest chronicles, most naval historians have concluded that the ships were not well armed. The work of Donald Keith, director of Ships of Discovery, and other nautical archaeologists has challenged that view. Dr. Keith reports that the earliest Caribbean shipwrecks have well-formed batteries of armament. For example, the Molasses Reef wreck, a late-fifteenth- to early-sixteenth-century Spanish wreck in the Turks & Caicos Islands, carried "ship-killing" wrought-iron cannons, swivel guns mounted on the "gunwale" (hence the name), smaller swivel guns called harquebuts, and a variety of portable arms including rifles, crossbows, lances, swords, and even hand grenades. These weapons show a sophisticated appreciation of guns. They certainly were a key element in the conquest of the Americas.

These were not, however, warships. The warships of the day were galleys, long, sleek vessels driven to sea by an oversize sail and then propelled into battle by scores of oarsmen. Their bows were constructed as battlefields with a battering ram leading the way below an artillery platform, from which large-caliber cannons fired scrap metal, and a boarding platform, from which archers, musketeers, and swivel gunners attacked the enemy from close range.

The ships of exploration were general-purpose cargo vessels called "caravels" (investors were reluctant to risk first-class ships). They were uncomfortable and were not made for the business of discovery, yet their maneuverability, their flexibility of rigging, their ability to travel more than one hundred miles per day under favorable conditions, and to sail in shallow water gave them a major role in voyages of exploration.

25
A World on the Wax

Following the cycle of the moon, interest in the native peoples of the Caribbean has waxed and waned. At the time of the Columbus Quincentennary, the consensus among scholars was that the native peoples were extinct. The Taínos of the Greater Antilles were decimated by harsh treatment and the introduction of European diseases for which they had no immunities in the first decades of the sixteenth century, and neighboring peoples, like the Lucayan Taínos, were rounded up and enslaved as laborers in the gold mines of Hispaniola and the pearl-fishing industry of the southern Caribbean.

In the Lesser Antilles, the Island Caribs managed to hold off European efforts to colonize these islands for almost two hundred years. They did so by being more mobile and more bellicose in their response to British and French incursions in their territory, and through the brilliant political stategy of pitting one European power against the other. St. Lucia, for example, shifted between British and French suzerainty seventeen times during the early colonial period. When the French and British ceased fighting among themselves, their one enemy became the Island Caribs, and in 1797 the last remaining Caribs were captured, brought to St. Vincent, and then deported. The descendants of the Island Carib peoples living along the Moskito coast of Central America are today known as the Garifuna (Gonzáles 1988).

It would seem that by the beginning of the eighteenth century all of the native peoples had been exterminated. It is clear that Europeans succeeded in suppressing native lifeways and erasing their cultures within several generations. However, it is

40. Sunset behind the Pitons, St. Lucia. Photo by William F. Keegan.

not true that these societies left no imprint on subsequent historical developments in the islands. It is possible that some groups survived as refugees in remote locations, in much the same way as escaped slaves created maroon societies throughout the circum-Caribbean. As late as the nineteenth century, there were reports in Cuba of "wild Indians" raiding haciendas.

Well into the sixteenth century, most marriages in the Spanish islands (Cuba, the Dominican Republic, and Puerto Rico) were recorded as between Spanish men and Taíno women. Kathleen Deagan in her studies of the Spanish colonial enterprise, has documented the influence of Taíno women on the development of a "criollo" culture in the islands that blended Spanish and native ways of life. Caribbean culinary practices, fishing techniques, pottery vessels, housing, land use, and a wide variety of words (as we have shown in this volume) have survived to the present. Moreover, a recent study of mitochondrial DNA (which is passed to a child by its mother) showed that more than 60 percent of Puerto Ricans can trace their geneology to a Taíno woman.

Twenty years ago the Florida Museum of Natural History created a traveling museum exhibit called "First Encounters" (Milanich and Milbrath 1987). When the exhibit opened in Gainesville, Russell Means of the American Indian Movement and local sympathizers staged a protest in which they declared that "Columbus murdered a continent." Apparently, they had adopted the prevailing scholarly notion that the Taínos and Island Caribs were extinct.

We also need to recognize that twenty years ago the governments of many of the newly independent nations in the Caribbean also failed to recognize their native patrimony. For them, the main historical interest was their African heritage because the native peoples supposedly had contributed little to their modern legacy. In meeting with government representatives in Grenada in 1989, Keegan was told: "This Indian stuff is fine, but what about our heritage?"

The moon is waxing. There is a Carib reserve on the island of Dominica, and although these people do not live their lives like the Caribs of the sixteenth century, neither do we live the lives of our European ancestors. Cultures evolve. In Cuba, the Dominican Republic, and Puerto Rico especially, their Taíno heritage (patrimony) is now embraced. In fact, at the time of the Columbus Quincentennary, Fidel Castro declared that he was a Taíno (which is ironic given the hierarchical structure of Taíno societies in contrast to Castro's socialist ideals). Many other Caribbean nations now recognize the importance of their native heritage. Cultural patrimony is now protected on many islands where cultural resource management plans must be established before development is allowed to take place. Museums and heritage parks are growing apace throughout the region. The first peoples are being brought back to life, and as with all history it is alive and flourishing.

We have been blessed. We may be United States citizens by birth, but we are West Indian by choice. *The Times of the Islands,* The University of Alabama Press, and other publishers have given us the opportunity to bring the past to life. We are thrilled that others share our interest, and that the Caribbean peoples who have shared so much with us appreciate and share our interest in the cultural heritage of their islands.

Introduction to the Appendices

Words—(Between the Lines of Age*)

When we began writing these essays our premise was to use Taíno words to highlight the natural history of the Caribbean islands. The goal was to show continuities and discontinuities between the remote past and modern circumstances. Because they were published in the international magazine of the Turks & Caicos Islands (*Times of the Islands*) our essays had a particular focus on the Turks & Caicos. Nevertheless, we did not restrict our purview to these islands, and have tried to capture the broader sweep of Caribbean natural history.

Taíno words can be found scattered through the writings of the early Spanish chroniclers (Las Casas, Oviedo, Martyr, and others). Yet attempting to use a now-dead language (Harrison 2007) is a precarious proposition. The authors of this book are not linguists. As the Taíno did not have a written language, these are Spanish spellings for the words they heard, and they are not consistent. In addition, some words seem to be Spanish terms attributed to the Taínos. A good example is "pez reverso," the Taíno name for the remora fish according to Oviedo. This is clearly a Spanish term that does not fit typical Taíno orthography.

To a large degree we have been forced to rely on the scholarship of strangers. The most comprehensive collection of words was compiled by Luis Hernández Aquino (1977), who provided Spanish translations of mostly Taíno words. However, this dictionary must be used with caution because he also includes a number of words recorded by the Spanish in South and Central America. Thus, it is not strictly

*Neil Young (1971).

Taíno, although he usually does indicate the sources for the words that he includes. To complicate matters, this book is difficult to find. A more recent popular publication by Edwin Miner Solá (*Diccionario Taíno Illustrado,* 2002), provides a more user-friendly version that is profusely illustrated, although this, too, is in Spanish.

Hernández Aquino also suggests scientific names for most of the plants and animals in his lexicon. There are several problems with the scientific names that he selected. First, scientific taxonomy is continuously evolving so some of the names have been changed in the past thirty years. Second, some of the names are clearly inaccurate. In the appendices that follow we have offered our best guess at the scientific names for the plants and animals that have Taíno names.

The best discussion of Taíno language in English was written by Julian Granberry and Gary Vescelius (*Languages of the Pre-Columbian Antilles,* The University of Alabama Press 2004). We encourage anyone who is interested in talking Taíno to consult the phonetic spellings provided in this book. Speaking the language requires specific knowledge of translation and pronunciation. The Granberry and Vescelius book is especially useful because they break Taíno words into syllables that have particular meanings. These proved especially useful in Granberry's focus on place names (toponyms). The main shortcoming of this book is that it includes only an abbreviated list of words attributed to the Taíno language, and it largely ignores names for plants and animals.

In the appendices that follow we have included all of the Taíno words that we used to illustrate the natural history of the Caribbean prior to European contact. Our spellings, when possible, use the "source forms" recorded by Granberry and Vescelius. We recognize that there are multiple spellings for various words, but generally provide just one.

Words often have multiple meanings expressed in the subtleties of language. We are viewing the Taíno language and world through a Spanish filter. Our goal was not to create a dictionary of Taíno words, but rather to bring to life the worlds of the Taínos by recognizing those aspects of their lives that have been recorded in WORDS (between the lines of age).

Appendix 1

Taíno Names for Fishes

Taíno Word	Scientific Name	Common Name
Anguila	*Anguilla rostrata*	American eel (freshwater)
Bajonao	*Calamus bajonao*	Jolthead porgy
Balaju	*Hyporhampus unifasciatus*	Halfbeak
Bonasí	*Mycteroperca bonaci*	Black grouper
Buyón	*Scarus "lineolatus"* (*Sparisoma viride?*)	Esteemed parrotfish (Spotlight parrotfish?)
Cachicata	*Haemulon* sp.	Grunt
Cachuco	*Etelis oculatus*	Queen snapper
Caconeta	*none given*	Shark
Cajaya	*Carcharhinus leucas*	Bull shark
Caji	*Lutjanus apodus*	Schoolmaster
Carite	*Galeocerdo cuvier*	Tiger shark
Chibi	*Caranx ruber*	Bar jack
Chucho	*Aetobatus narinari*	Spotted eagle ray
Cojinua	*Caranx crysos*	Blue runner
Corocoro	*Haemulon macrostomum*	Spanish grunt
Dajao	*Agonostomus monticola*	Mountain mullet (freshwater)

Taíno Word	Scientific Name	Common Name
Diahaca	*Anisotremus surinamensis*	Black margate
Guabina	*Gobiomorus dormitator*	Bigmouth sleeper (freshwater)
Guacamaya	*Scarus guacamaia*	Rainbow parrotfish
Guaicáno or *Guaicán*	*Echeneis naucrates*	Remora or sharksucker
Guajil	*Mycteroperca venenosa*	Yellowfin grouper
Guaraguao	*Dactylopterus volitans*	Flying gurnard
Guaseta or *Guasa*	*Serranus* sp. or *Epinephelus* sp.	Sea bass/grouper
Guativere	Tripterygiidae	Blennies
Guavina	Pomacentridae or Synodontidae	Damselfish or lizardfish
Guaymen	*Caranx bartholomaei*	Yellow jack
Hagueta	none given	Small shark
Jallao	*Haemulon album*	Margate
Jarea	*Mugil curema*	White mullet
Jiguagua or *Area*	*Caranx hippos*	Crevalle jack
Jocú	*Lutjanus jocu*	Dog snapper
Libuza	*Dasyatis americana*	Southern stingray
Macabí or *Chiro*	*Elops saurus*	Ladyfish
Macurí	*Lobotes surinamensis*	Tripletail
Manjua	Atherinidae/Clupeidae/ Engraulididae	Silversides; herrings; anchovies
Mapiro or *Masaguan*	*Dormitator maculatus*	Fat sleeper (freshwater)
Mapo	*Rachycentron canadum?*	Cobia?
Mijúa	*Jenkinsia lamprotaenia*	Dwarf round herring
Moharra or *Mojarra*	*Diplodus vulgaris*	Seabream
Muniama	*Pristipomoides macrophtha-lamus*	Cardinal snapper
Muniama de afuera	*Eucinostomus* sp.	Mojarra; jenny
Oatilibi	*Bodianus rufus*	Spanish hogfish
Paguala	*Chaetodipterus faber*	Atlantic spadefish

Taíno Word	Scientific Name	Common Name
Pargo	*Lutjanus purpureus*	Caribbean red snapper
Patán	*Gerres cinereus*	Yellowfin mojarra
Peto	*Acanthocybium solandri*	Wahoo
Sabalo	*Megalops atlanticus*	Tarpon
Sesí	*Lutjanus buccanella*	Blackfin snapper
Setí	*Gobionellus oceanicus*	Highfin goby (freshwater)
Sirajo	*Sycidium plumieri*	Sirajo in Gobiidae family (freshwater)

Primary source: Hernández Aquino 1977.

Appendix 2

Taíno Names for Animals

TAÍNO WORD	SCIENTIFIC NAME	COMMON NAME
Mammals		
Aguti or *Guimo*	*Dasyprocta agouti*	Agouti
Hutia or *Jutia*	Capromidae	Hutia
Manati	*Trichechus manatus*	Manatee
Quemi or *Cori*	*Cavia porcellus*	Guinea pig
Invertebrates		
Burgao	none given	Intertidal mollusk
Buruguena	*Epilabocera sinuatifrons*	River crab
Caguara	none given	Clam (to cut hair)
Carrucho or *Cobo*	*Strombus gigas*	Queen conch
Chagara or *Guabara*	*Atya scabra*	Shrimp (freshwater)
Cocolia	*Callinectes sapidus*	Blue crab
Donaca	*Donax denticulatus*	"Chip-chip"; coquina clam
Guamo	*Charonia variegata*	Atlantic triton's trumpet
Jaiba	*Callinectes diacanthus*	Blue crab
Juey	*Cardisoma guanhumi*	Blue land crab

Taíno Word	Scientific Name	Common Name
Reptiles and Lizards		
Ameiva	*Ameiva* sp.	Teiid lizard
Anoli	*Anolis* sp.	Anole lizard
Bayoya or *Caguaya*	*Leiocephalus* sp.	Curly-tail lizard
Caguama	*Chelonia mydas*	Green sea turtle
Carey	*Eretmochelys imbricata*	Hawksbill sea turtle
Fandusca or *Fanduca*	*Dermochelys coriacea*	Leatherback sea turtle
Galapago	*Geochelone* sp.	Land tortoise
Hicotea or *Jicotea*	*Trachemys* sp.	Freshwater turtle
Higuana or *Jiguana*	*Cyclura* sp.	Rock iguana
Maja	*Epicrates* sp.	Boa
Birds		
Ani	*Crotophaga ani*	Smooth-billed ani
Aura	*Cathartes aura*	Turkey vulture
Bajani	*Columba passerina*	Ground dove
Bijirita	*Dendroica adelaidae*	Adelaide's warbler
Capacho	*Loxigilla portoricensis*	Puerto Rican bullfinch
Caracara	*Falconidae*	Falcon; caracara
Carrao	*Aramus guarauna*	Limpkin
Curua	*Phalacrocorax olivaceus*	Olivaceus cormorant
Cuyaya	*Falco sparverius*	American kestrel
Guabairo	*Caprimulgus vociferus*	Nightjar or whip-poor-will
Guacamayo	*Ara* sp.	Macaw
Guacarigua	*Trochilidae*	Hummingbird
Guagaica	*Saurothera vieilloti*	Puerto Rican lizard cuckoo
Guanana	*Anser caerulescens*	Snow goose
Guaraguao	*Buteo platypterus*	Broad-tailed hawk
Guatibiri	*Tyrannus dominicensis*	Gray kingbird
Guincho	*Pandion haliaetus*	Osprey
Higuaca	*Amazona vittata*	Puerto Rican parrot
Inriri	*Melanerpes portoricensis*	Puerto Rican woodpecker
Jajabi	*Aratinga* sp.	Small parrot; parakeet
Jui	*Myiarchus* sp.	Flycatcher
Mucaro	*Otis nudipes*	Puerto Rican screech owl

Taíno Word	Scientific Name	Common Name
Mucaro real and Mucarode sabana	*Asio flammeus*	Short-eared owl
Querequete	*Chordeiles minor*	Common nighthawk
Quisquidi	*Vireo latimeri*	Puerto Rican vireo
Sabanero	*Charadrius vociferus*	Killdeer
Sora	*Porzana carolina*	Sora
Tujuy	*Fulica caribea*	Caribbean coot
Yaboa comun	*Nyctanassa violacea*	Yellow-crown night heron
Yaboa real	*Nycticorax nycticorax*	Black-crowned night heron
Yaboa americana	*Botaurus lentiginosus*	American bittern
Yaguasa	*Ardea herodias*	Great blue heron
Yegua	*Rallus longirostris*	Clapper rail
Yeguete	*Himantopus himantopus*	Common stilt

Primary source: Hernández Aquino 1977.

Appendix 3

Other Taíno Words

Taíno Word	Translation
Ababaia or *Papaya*	Papaya
Aji	Hot pepper (*Capsicum* sp.)
Anana or *Yayagua*	Pineapple
Aon	Dog
Arcabuco	Forest
Arieto/Ariete	Ceremonial song and dance
Ayiti	Hispaniola/Española; source of word "Haiti"
Baira	Bow (of a bow and arrow)
Baracutey	Solitary; barracuda
Barbacoa	Wooden lattice for smoking meats (barbecue)
Batey	Ball game
Behique	Shaman
Bija	Achiote
Bohio	Home
Boniata	Sweet potato
Burén	Ceramic griddle
Cabuya	fishing line
Cacicazgo	Chiefdom

Taíno Word	Translation
Cacique	Chief
Caico	Outer or faraway island; distant island
Caimito	Yellow sapote
Cairi	Small island
Caney	Conical house
Canoa	Dugout canoe
Caona	Reward; gold; heavenly wealth
Caribe	Mythical being from world of the dead
Carobei or Sarobey	Cotton plant
Casabi	Cassava bread
Casiripe	Pepper pot
Caya	"Towards island", pass between islands
Cayo	Small island (cay)
Cayuco	Flat boat with no keel (raft)
Cemí or Zemí	Deity or object that represents a deity
Chicha	Corn "beer"
Ciba	Stone or stony
Ciboney	Peoples of central Cuba
Cibucán	Basketry tube for squeezing manioc pulp
Ciguaya	People of the Samaná peninsula, the Dominican Republic
Coa	Digging stick
Cobo	Shell; "outer house"; conch
Cohoba	Narcotic snuff
Conuco	Agricultural field
Cuyo	Light
Duho	Chief's chair or stool
Gioia	Narcotic herb
Gua	"Our"; possible designation for a favored thing; saltwater
Guada	House garden
Guamo	Shell trumpet
Guanábana	Soursop
Guanahacabibe	Small land of caves
Guanahaní	Columbus's first landfall (San Salvador)
Guanahatabey	People of western Cuba
Guani	Bee hummingbird
Guayaba	Guava

Taíno Word	Translation
Guayo	Grater board
Guey	Sun
Guiro	Gourd or calabash
Haba	Basket
Hamaca	Hammock
Henequen	Sisal
Huracán	Powerful storm (hurricane)
Jagua	Genipap
Jaojao	Finest quality cassava bread
Jejen or *Maye*	Mosquito
Jico or *Hico*	Rope or cord to hang hammock
Jujo	Small snake
Karaya	Moon
Li	He, belonging to him
Liza	Large grouper
Lu	Tribe or people
Lucairi	Island people
Maca	Large tree for making canoe
Macana	War club
Maguay	Wooden drum
Mahiz	Corn
Makuto	Deep basket
Mamey	Mamey apple
Mani or *Cacahuete*	Peanut
Mapu	Large, red tree
Maraca	Gourd rattle
Montone	Agricultural mound
Naboria	Class of servants
Nahe	Paddle
NiTaíno	Elites or noble class
Opía	Spirit of the dead
Pez reverso	Remora
Piragua	Carib canoe with sail
Potala	Stone net weight
Potiza	Ceramic water bottle
Robalo	Grouper
Sabana	Savannah

Taíno Word	Translation
Tabaco	Tobacco
Taíno	Noble or good person
Tuna	Prickly pear fruit
Turey	Gold, sky, heavenly
Uicu	Cassava "beer"
Xara	Lake
Xawei	Sinkhole
Xaweye	Cave
Yabisi	Fruit or shade tree
Yacayeque	Village
Yuca	Manioc
Zum-zum	Hummingbird

Bibliography

Arrom, Juan José. *Mitología y Artes Prehispánicas de las Antillas.* Mexico: Siglo XXI Editores, 1975.

Arrom, Juan José, ed. *Fray Ramón Pané, Relación Acerca de las Antigüedades de los Indios: el Primer Tratado Escrito en América.* Mexico: Siglo XXI Editores, 1974.

Bligh, William, Edward Christian, and R. D. Madison. *The Bounty Mutiny.* London: Penguin Classics, 2001.

Bond, James. *Birds of the West Indies.* New York: Houghton Mifflin, 1961.

Breton, Raymond. *Dictionnaire caröibe-français.* Auxerre: Giles Bouquet, 1665.

Brinton, Daniel. The Arawak Language of Guiana and Its Linguistic and Ethnological Relations. *Transactions of the American Philosophical Society* 14 (1871): 427–444.

Budinoff, Linda C. An Osteological Analysis of the Human Burials Recovered from Maisabel: An Early Ceramic Site on the North Coast of Puerto Rico. In *Proceedings of the 12th Congress of the International Association for Caribbean Archaeology,* ed. L. S. Robinson. A.I.A.C., Martinique: A.I.A.C., 1991. Pp. 117–134.

Carlson, Lisabeth A. Strings of Command: Manufacture and Utilization of Shell Beads among the Taíno Indians of the West Indies. M.A. thesis, Department of Anthropology, University of Florida, Gainesville, 1993.

Carlson, Lisabeth A. Aftermath of a Feast: Human Colonization of the Southern Bahamian Archipelago and Its Effects on the Indigenous Fauna. Ph.D. dissertation, Department of Anthropology, University of Florida, Gainesville, 1999.

Conrad, Geoff W., John W. Foster, and Charles D. Beeker. Organic Artifacts from Mantanial de la Aleta, Dominican Republic: Preliminary Observations and Interpretations. *Journal of Caribbean Archaeology* 2 (2000): 1–20.

Craton, Michael, and Gail Saunders. *Islanders in the Stream: A History of the Bahamian People. Volume One: From Aboriginal Times to the End of Slavery.* Athens: University of Georgia Press, 1992.

Crosby, Alfred. *The Columbian Exchange.* Westport, CT: Greenwood Press, 1972.

Davis, E. Wade. *The Serpent and the Rainbow.* New York: Simon & Schuster, 1997.

Deagan, Kathleen, and José Maria Cruzent. *Archaeology at La Isabela: America's First European Town.* New Haven, CT: Yale University Press, 2002.

Dunn, Oliver, and James E. Kelley Jr., eds. *The Diario of Christopher Columbus's First Voyage to America, 1492–1493 (abstracted by Bartholomé de las Casas).* Norman: University of Oklahoma Press, 1989.

Fuson, Robert. *The Log of Christopher Columbus.* Camden, ME: International Marine Publishing, 1987.

González, Nancie L. Solien. *Sojourners of the Caribbean: Ethnogenesis and Ethnohistory of the Garifuna.* Urbana: University of Illinois Press, 1988.

Granberry, Julian. The Cultural Position of the Bahamas in Caribbean Archaeology. *American Antiquity* 22 (1956): 128–134.

Granberry, Julian, and Gary Vescelius. *Languages of the Pre-Columbian Antilles.* Tuscaloosa: The University of Alabama Press, 2004.

Harrison, K. David. *When Languages Die: The Extinction of the World's Languages and the Erosion of Human Knowledge.* Oxford: Oxford University Press, 2007.

Henige, David. *In Search of Columbus: The Sources for the First Voyage.* Tempe: University of Arizona Press, 1991.

Hernández Aquino, Luis. *Diccionario de voces indígenas de Puerto Rico.* 2nd edition. Puerto Rico: Editorial Cultural, 1977.

Hobbes, Thomas. *Leviathan.* Oxford: Oxford University Press, 1998; orig. pub. 1651.

Hurston, Zora Neale. *Tell My Horse: Voodoo and Life in Haiti and Jamaica.* New York: Harper & Row, 1990 (originally published in 1938).

Irving, Washington. *The Life and Voyages of Christopher Columbus.* Boston: Twayne Publishers, 1981.

Keegan, William F. *The People Who Discovered Columbus.* Gainesville: University Press of Florida, 1992.

Keegan, William F. *Bahamian Archaeology: Life in the Bahamas and Turks & Caicos Before Columbus.* Nassau: Media Publishing, 1997.

Keegan William F. History and Culture of Food and Drink in the Americas, Section V.D.2. The Caribbean, Including Northern South America and Eastern Central America: Early History. In *The Cambridge World History of Food,* ed. Kipple, K., and K. C. Ornelas. Cambridge: Cambridge University Press, 2000. Pp. 1260–1277.

Keegan, William F. *Taíno Indian Myth and Practice: The Arrival of the Stranger King.* Gainesville: University Press of Florida, 2007.

Keen, Benjamin, trans. *The Life of Admiral Christopher Columbus by His Son Ferdinand.* New Brunswick, N.J.: Rutgers University Press, 1959.

Kipple, Kenneth, and K. C. Ornelas, eds. *The Cambridge World History of Food.* Cambridge: Cambridge University Press, 2000.

Las Casas, Bartolomé de. *Historia de las Indias.* 3 volumes, ed. A. Millares Carlo. Mexico City: Fondo de Cultura Económica, 1951.

London, Jack. *John Barleycorn.* Elibron Classics, Adamant Media Corporation, 2006 (originally published in 1913).

Lovén, Sven. *Origins of the Tainan Culture, West Indies.* Goteborg, Sweden: Elanders Boktryckeri Aktiebolag, 1935.

Maples, William R., and Michael Browning. *Dead Men Do Tell Tales.* New York: Doubleday, 1994.

Martir de Angleria, Pedro. *Decadas del Nuevo Mundo, 2 vols.* Santo Domingo: Sociedad Domini-
cana de Bibliofilos Inc., 1989.
Martyr D'Anghiera, Peter. *De Orbe Novo [1493–1525].* Translated by F. A. MacNutt. New York:
Burt Franklin, 1970.
Meggers, Betty. *Amazonia: Man and Culture in a Counterfeit Paradise.* Washington: Smithsonian
Institution Press, 1996.
Milanich, Jerald, and Susan Milbrath, eds. *First Encounters: Spanish Explorations in the Caribbean
and the United States, 1492–1570.* Gainesville: University Press of Florida, 1989.
Miner Solá, Edwin. Diccionario *Taíno Illustrado.* Serie: Puerto Rico Prehistorico, vol. 1. Puerto
Rico: Ediciones Servilibro, 2002.
Montaigne, Michel de. *The Essays of Montaigne.* Translated by J. Florino, 3 vols. New York: AMS
Press, 1967 (originally published in 1580).
Morison, Samuel Eliot. *Admiral of the Ocean Sea.* Boston: Little, Brown and Company, 1942.
Naipaul, Shiva. *The Chip-Chip Gatherers.* New York: Alfred A. Knopf, 1973.
Newsom, Lee Ann, and Elizabeth S. Wing. *On Land and Sea: Native American Uses of Biological
Resources in the West Indies.* Tuscaloosa: The University of Alabama Press, 2004.
Oviedo y Valdés, Gonzalo Fernández de. *Historia General y Natural de las Indias, vols. 1–2.* Ma-
drid: Ediciones Atlas, 1959.
Pares, Richard. *War and Trade in the West Indies.* London: F. Cass, 1963.
Price, Richard. Caribbean Fishing and Fisherman: A Historical Sketch. *American Anthropolo-
gist* 68 (1996): 1363–1383.
Quamman, David. *The Song of the Dodo.* New York: Simon & Schuster, 1996.
Randall, John E. *Caribbean Reef Fishes.* Neptune City, NJ: T. F. H. Publications, 1968.
Roe, P. G. Just Wasting Away: Taíno Shamanism and Concepts of Fertility. In *Taíno: Pre-
Columbian Art and Culture from the Caribbean,* ed. F. Bercht, E. Brodsky, J. A. Farmer, and
D. Taylor. New York: Monacelli Press, 1997. Pp. 124–157.
Rouse, Irving. *The Taínos: The People Who Greeted Columbus.* New Haven, CT: Yale University
Press, 1992.
Sahlins, Marshall. *Stone Age Economics.* Chicago: Aldine, 1972.
Sahlins, Marshall. *Islands of History.* Chicago: University of Chicago Press, 1985.
Sale, Kirckpatrick. *The Conquest of Paradise: Columbus and the Columbian Legacy.* New York:
Knopf, 1990.
Sauer, Carl O. *The Early Spanish Main.* Berkeley and Los Angeles: University of California Press,
1966.
Scarry, Margaret C., and Elizabeth J. Reitz. Herbs, Fish, Scum, and Vermin: Subsistence Strate-
gies in Sixteenth-century Spanish Florida. In *Columbian Consequences, Vol. 2: Archaeological
and Historical Perspectives in the Spanish Borderlands East,* ed. David Hurst Thomas. Wash-
ington, D.C.: Smithsonian Institution Press, 1990. Pp. 343–354.
Scudder, Sylvia. Evidence of Sea Level Rise at the Early Ostionan Coralie Site (GT-3), c. AD
700, Grand Turk, Turks & Caicos Islands. *Journal of Archaeological Science* 28 (2001): 1221–
1233.
Sealey, Neil E. *Bahamian Landscapes.* London: Collins Caribbean, 1985.
Sears, William H., and Shaun D. Sullivan. Bahamas Archaeology. *American Antiquity* 43 (1978):
3–25.
Siegel, Peter E. Ideology, Power, and Social Complexity in Prehistoric Puerto Rico. Ph.D. disser-
tation, State University of New York, Binghamton, 1992.
Sinelli, Peter T. Archaeological Investigations of Two Prehistoric Sites Representing Hispaniolan

Colonization of Middle Caicos, Turks & Caicos Islands. MA thesis, University of Florida, Gainesville, 2001.

Steadman, David. *Extinction and Biogeography of Tropical Pacific Birds.* Chicago: University of Chicago Press, 2006.

Stevens-Arroyo, Antonio M. *Cave of the Jagua: The Mythological World of the Taínos.* Albuquerque: University of New Mexico Press, 1988.

Stokes, Anne V. A Biogeographic Survey of Prehistoric Human Diet in the West Indies Using Stable Isotope Analysis. Ph.D. dissertation, University of Florida, Gainesville, 1998.

Sullivan, Shaun D. The Colonization and Exploitation of the Turks & Caicos Islands. Ph.D. dissertation, University of Illinois at Urbana-Champaign, 1981.

Theroux, Paul. *Sir Vidia's Shadow.* New York: Mariner Books, 1998.

Truss, Lynne. *Eats, Shoots, and Leaves.* New York: Gotham Books, 2003.

Valcárcel Rojas, Roberto, and César A. Rodríguez Arce. El Chorro de Maíta: Social Inequality and Mortuary Space. In *Dialogues in Cuban Archaeology,* ed. L. Antonio Curet. Tuscaloosa: The University of Alabama Press, 2004.

Van Sertima, Ivan. *African Presence in Early America.* New Brunswick, NJ: Transaction Publishers, 1992.

Veloz Maggiolo, Marcio. *Panorama histórico del Caribe precolombino.* Edición del Banco Central de la República Dominicana, Santo Domingo, 1991.

Veloz Maggiolo, Marcio. *La Isla de Santo Domingo antes de Colon.* Banco Central de la República Dominicana, Santo Domingo, 1993.

West, D. C., and A. Kling. *The Libro de las Profecias of Christopher Columbus.* Gainesville: University Press of Florida, 1991.

Whitehead, Neil, ed. *Wolves from the Sea: Readings in the Anthropology of the Native Caribbean.* Leiden: KITLV Press, 1995.

Wilkie, Laurie, and Paul Farnsworth. *Sampling Many Pots: An Archaeology of Memory and Tradition at a Bahamian Plantation.* Gainesville: University Press of Florida, 2005.

Index